RE-DISCOVERING
THE
SACRED

RE-DISCOVERING THE SACRED

Spirituality in America

PHYLLIS A. TICKLE

CROSSROAD · NEW YORK

1995

The Crossroad Publishing Company
370 Lexington Avenue, New York, NY 10017

Copyright © 1995 by Phyllis A. Tickle

Printed in the United States of America

Library of Congress Cataloging-in-Publication Data

Tickle, Phyllis.
    Re-discovering the sacred : Spirituality in America / Phyllis
Tickle.
      p. cm.
    ISBN 0-8245-1460-2
    1. United States—Religion—1960- I. Title. II. Title:
Rediscovering the sacred spirituality in America.
BL2525.T53 1995
200'.973—dc20   95-1368
                                         CIP

IN MEMORIAM

June Chumley Ward
1932–1994

Contents

Preface

RELIGION, THE SPIRITUAL, AND THE SACRED are big business in America, there being quite literally hundreds of thousands of us gainfully employed every day in the service of one or another or all three. By my own informal tally, the three account as well for at least two thousand distinct job descriptions and positions. Of all of those myriad positions and job descriptions, however, mine is, so far as I can tell, absolutely singular. I began some time ago, in fact, to describe my job as being more or less like life in the catbird seat. I still tend to see it in that way.

Publishers Weekly is not a magazine that one sees lying about in doctors' offices or carefully spread about on low tables in most business foyers. It is instead an international trade journal serving the book industry from librarians and booksellers to writers and publishers, rights buyers, reporters, and everybody else in between. *PW,* to call it by its more familiar name, serves America's readers, in other words, by serving well the industry that conceptualizes and then realizes the books that are our common culture as well as our entertainment and continuity; but *PW* itself remains fairly invisible except to the dedicated book reader who scans book advertisements and book jackets to see if and what *PW* may have said about a book before deciding whether to buy that book.

As religion editor for *PW,* my job is to see in manuscript and/or bound galleys the English-language books in religion, spirituality, and sacred literature that are to be published within, usually, a year of my first receiving them. Out of that mass of books-to-be, my responsibility is first to select for review those materials

9

that seem most worthy of our attention, most likely to find a large and hungry audience, and/or most significant in terms of their potential contribution to our national life. Second, it is my job to identify shifts in the market, in areas and genres of public interest, in editorial trends and the like, and having done so, to cover those shifts in such a way as hopefully to render them into useful diagnostic and prognostic information for the bookseller, the librarian, the writer, the editor, the publisher, the rights buyer, the media reporter, and ultimately, if indirectly, the bookbuying reader.

What one discovers in the course of that kind of daily occupation is a great deal about religion, the sacred, and the spiritual in America right now and a fair amount about those same three for the months beyond right now. What one discovers — and indeed must discover — is the patterns of faith and practice that actually appertain among us. The data about how many of us are reading what at what cost in time and dollars within which areas of religion, spirituality, and the sacred become a kind of template that gives objective clarification to what is at its most articulate still a subjective terrain.

I came to this job, as do most religionists, out of a lifelong, personal absorption with the sacred, the spiritual, and the religious; and I am pleased, on good days anyway, to regard my being here as a vocation in both the mundane and the theological sense of that word. Unlike most religionists, however, I rarely get a chance to share with the world at large either my passion for the life of faith or my understanding of what it means in the lives of most of us. This book is my attempt to change that situation. This book is, in other words, a view from the catbird seat.

PHYLLIS TICKLE

– 1 –

Where We Are

Lord Jesus Christ, Son of God, have mercy on me, a sinner.
Lord Jesus Christ, Son of God, have mercy on me, a sinner.
Lord Jesus Christ, Son of God, have mercy on me, a sinner.

THE WORDS ARE THOSE of the Jesus Prayer. Aside from the Our Father, they are the oldest prayer in the Christian tradition and most assuredly the oldest to come up into the West out of solely human authorship. They are also the most powerful words in my day-to-day experience, though I do not even pretend to understand completely why that is so.

I do know that for centuries orthodox believers taught their children the Jesus Prayer in infancy, urging them to repeat it frequently at random times during both the day and the wakeful moments of their nights. I know that, at least among the religiously innocent, it once was used (and perhaps still is, perhaps even still is by me) as much as magical incantation as credo or petition. I know that the Prayer, like many another distillate of civilized spiritual experience, was not welcome in the rural Protestantism of my Christian grandparents and great-grandparents. Among them, there was neither time nor strength enough for individual souls to assume responsibility for themselves. Rather, to survive the frontier's necessities, my American forebears resigned themselves to authority, apparently mistrusting spiritual deviation as genuinely as I now mistrust its counterpart of conformity.

Because I understand the exigencies of that former time, I can forgive its causes as well as its consequences; yet the fact still remains that because of those exigencies, I came to the Jesus Prayer not in childhood, as should have been my baptismal right, but in adulthood. I came to it long after I had learned about mantras and breath control, about daily offices, and about the spiritual disciplines of meditation, fasting, and prayer. It was this having gone around the barn only to come in through the backdoor, so to speak, by means of the Jesus Prayer that finally exposed to me in adulthood both the singular and mystical richness of the Christian life itself and also, as antecedent to that life, the distinction that must be made between the sacred and the religious in human living.

There is a material difference between the sacred and the religious, although most of us approach them as contiguous territories. This fact, as I have said, was lost on me until I discovered, almost by accident, the Jesus Prayer. The prayer (like so many of my generation and kind, I found it in a book — God be thanked for books!) is not a mantra. No, the Jesus Prayer is not that sweet, consoling single syllable that seduces consciousness and at least briefly releases it away from itself. The Jesus Prayer is, when all is said and done, still a prayer, as much petition and confession as formula, but a mantric prayer. Because it is mantric, it moves the attention to the sacred and shifts the intellect toward the heart; yet because it is also credo and profession, the prayer moves the pray-er to religion.

It is not, however, with religious profession that I want presently to be occupied. Instead, I would have us investigate that which the Jesus Prayer bridges. I would have us stop awhile with the sacred and occupy ourselves with how it may be discovered, this wonderful country of the subjective world where we learn to love each other beyond judgmentalism or creeds. I would have us, ultimately, to discover the sacred. And should that discovery take some of us, my own life's experience included, on into religion, then that too is agreeable to the exercise. But the sacred is, of the two, the one that is common to all men and women, accessible to all humanity. And while no religion, I suspect, is possible for those who refuse to acknowledge and traverse the sacred, it is still true that religion itself is not essential to human existence. The sacred, on the other hand, like the sun, one's cardiovascular system, or our human capacity for imagination, simply is. And by virtue of that characteristic, the sacred is not very subject to human choice, although it may clearly be victimized by some of the choices we make.

Religion, for most of us, is an attitude for interpreting history, both the massive, collective history of our species in general and the private histories of our own small existences. Religion is also a governor we set upon our choices, upon both our large societal choices and upon our small individual choices. Religion gives point and purpose to the confusion of our foreshortened view of life, although sometimes, ironically, it does so to the diminution and denigration of the sacred. But religion, whether we are comfortable admitting it or not, is as much a man-made construct as a god-made one. It is, in the popular terminology of our day, at its core a co-creation between the mystery of immutable absolutes and our attempts to engage, apply, manipulate, appease, and enjoin those absolutes. The sacred, however, submits to nothing. It is.

The sacred is a structural given in our being, very much indeed like one's cardiovascular system or the sun that for so many human eons has served as symbol to the sacred. Like those things, the sacred can be perceived but never embraced, for it and they are as fundamentally and inextricably woven into life as its perfume is into a flower or its meaning is into a word. Yet just as we know ourselves to have moved into and through the perfume of the sweet spring daffodils or to have named and passed on an articulated idea, so too we know when we have "moved" into the sacred, for the sacred is most frequently referenced by us as geography.

It is the words and metaphors of place with which we discuss the sacred and by means of which we see ourselves as able to engage it; although at the very moment in which we speak of that "otherness," as another world, we know in ourselves the hollowness of such a naming, for the sacred is "place" as no earth place is. Like the womb that we cannot remember, the sacred is itself. Its placeness is its aliveness, and all our words are thereby frustrated. Weary of too much trying, we finally fall back upon natural geography and talk, half angrily at times, about paths and journeys and quests, about states of being and realms, the City of God, Paradise and the garden of beginning, the wonderland on the other side of the mirror, the land of Narnia, and Tolkien's mountain. The list is endless. But it is all geography, all the vocabulary and symbolic reductions of geography, and all of the reductions as perfectly accurate as they are inadequate; yet we can do no better.

So the sacred then is, for us in our limitations, a world apart, a living place in the body of living that is both the containing and the contained. It is a garden, well tended and dew cleansed. Or it is the cleared and sun-warmed piazza of an alabaster palace. Or it is a fecund, calm jungle with bowered paths and still pools; or the secrecy of a favored copse filled with the half-light of cool, moist greens and the dark crevices of shadow. But always — whatever the image of the heart's moment — always the sacred is a place of strange community where what communes lacks body but exists and is perceived as personed, the whole sweetness of its communion being as nondiscursive as music and as understandable.

The sacred is an essence perceived as a place wherein all that can be grasped is equally present, where the good and the evil have changed to the warm and the cold, and neither is better; a place where light and its absence are the emotions. It is a place where we know ourselves as hollow, open-ended tubes whose hollowness too is as it must be, just as surely as the separate flutes of a pipe must likewise be unknowing and ungrasping of themselves; a place of commonality, for commonality is and is only outside of time; a place of restful abandonment, for no struggle is valid save that which lies beyond the will and can be neither advanced nor avoided by means of the will; a place of the ordinary and of the very old, both forever fixed in the vitality and sanctity of their own agedness and domestic mundanity. The sacred is, in other words, home.

But just as the Buddhist koan reminds us that the eye can never see itself, so home is that which we cannot perceive so long as we remain a part of it. "Home," like the sacred, is a locative understanding born of severance and only viewable through the yearning lens of loss. The child has home and does not know it; the adult does not have home and constantly knows it. Who can say which is better? Both circumstances are inevitable in our sense of home and so too in our discovering of the sacred.

– 2 –

Why We Are in Turmoil

TO TRACK THE SACRED STATISTICALLY is so quintessentially American — so perfectly exemplary of our national penchant for reducing poetry to audience size and number of books sold — that I chuckle as well as cringe every time I catch myself or someone else doing it. Quantification, however, disciplines personal opinion, and even in sacred matters accuracy has its place. The irony, of course, is that no one, not even the most accomplished statistician, can "get at" the sacred. All he or she can do is measure the presentations of the sacred, all those observable actions and objective statements of belief that we recognize as growing out of the subjective life and, by declension, out of our engagement with the sacred.

Of the measurable human activities that manifest sacral realities, the most observable, and therefore the most quantifiable, is obviously religious practice. The second, more statistically suspect because it is more subjective, is spirituality,[1] both as an attitude about the sacred and as a set of personal choices and disciplines for living in accord with it.[2] If we want to know about the presence of the sacred in contemporary America, therefore, we usually look at the spirituality and the religious practices with which most of us evidence that presence.[3] But there is another, subtler, way as well of gauging our involvement just as (God help us as a culture!) one really can track the course of poetry by tracking the size and characteristics of its audience and the number and types of poetry books sold.[4]

Books and book types are a very defensible tool, in fact, for describing what really is happening, has happened, and can reasonably be expected to happen in almost any part of our national life, including most particularly spirituality and religion. There are probably several good reasons for that, but two seem to me to be especially compelling.

Books looked at in overview at a national level; books looked at in terms of patterns of bestsellers and inventory flow; books looked at in terms of projected trends as discovered by publisher and distributor research — books in that context are diagnostic not of what we as Mr., Mrs., and Ms. America *say* we are doing but of what we *really* are doing, with our time and inside our respective interiors. That kind of bypassing of personal defenses is the first reason that books are honest demographers.

The second reason is that all human beings are slow to change their public and social ways. As a species, we are especially slow to express aloud religious beliefs or visibly to pursue religious patterns that are too divergent from those of our community. We go public as a rule only after we are assured of finding some replacement group within our new practices, or else — rarely — we are completely overwhelmed by some incontrovertible personal conviction. Books, although they are a modern comfort and only recently available inexpensively and readily, are private. Books don't tell, especially in matters of the spirit. What the soul sends the mind in search of can be explored without prejudice in a book, and almost as significant, what the mind finds can then be checked, and evaluated, and tested against another book, and another, and another, ad infinitum and all with an almost perfect impunity.

Individual books tell no individual secrets, in other words; but in aggregate they can expose a landscape.[5] And what books currently are establishing about our landscape is, first and foremost, a burgeoning and generalized absorption with spirituality and religion in America today.[6] Because the book industry monitors itself so carefully (one could even say so obsessively), there are quite literally dozens of proofs available for such a statement, but two or three can easily serve as representative of them all.

Books move to market from a publisher to a sales outlet via a number of avenues, wholesalers being the largest single channel of delivery; and among American book wholesalers, by far the largest is the Ingram Book Company.[7] When in mid-1994 Ingram announced its intention to further expand its religion/spirituality inventory, senior vice president of marketing, Larry Carpenter, explained the company's decision. "In the last twelve months," Carpenter said, "Ingram has enjoyed a 249 percent growth in the movement of religion product," a growth index that would be remarkable in any context.

Shortly before the Ingram announcement, in February 1994, the Association of American Publishers, which also tracks the movement of books very carefully, had already reported that the sales of books in the Bible/religion/spirituality category were up 59 percent nationally over sales for February 1992. Earlier, in June 1992, *American Bookseller*, the official publication of the American Booksellers Association, had devoted six pages to this emerging pattern, declaring that "the category's expansion is indisputable."[8] An even earlier Gallup study had projected that the largest sales increase in nonfiction books in the twenty-first century would be in religion/spirituality books (82 percent growth by 2010 over 1987), to be followed at a considerable distance (59 percent) by second-place investment/economic/income tax books. As if in preparation for that predicted pattern, the American Booksellers Association in 1995 opened for the first time a special section of its annual convention and trade show for what it categorizes as "religious/spiritual/inspirational" books.

Within the past two or three years various bestseller lists have also begun for the first time to confirm the same predictions and establish them as being more than theoretical, showing religion/spirituality titles able to consistently perform alongside (and sometimes outperform) secular titles on general lists.[9] In a special May 29, 1994 ABA supplement of *USA Today,* for instance, Deirdre Donahue, *USA*'s book publishing reporter since 1986, talked about her paper's then relatively new bestseller listings. "I am still surprised," she wrote, "by what will top the list on any given day. For example, I am surprised that spiritual books...have become such big sellers."

Using book sales as a tool for documenting America's growing involvement with the sacred has likewise become an accepted practice among the national media during the nineties. In July 1991, for example, *Business Week* quietly observed that sales from the five thousand retail stores that belong to the Christian Booksellers Association (CBA) alone had risen from $1 billion in 1980 to $2.7 billion by 1990. Such observations, however, were little more than early acknowledgments of something already in process.[10] The precursors of our present preoccupation with spirituality and religion stretch farther back than the late eighties in which it began to be visible and have to do with audience, both lay and professional, as well as with books.

Barbara DeConcini, executive director of the American Academy of Religion, the chief learned society dedicated to the academic study of religion, for example, has gone on record saying that "the academic study of religion, it is fair to say, has enjoyed something of a renaissance during the last thirty years."[11] Most observers agree with the correctness of DeConcini's timetable, not only for university classrooms but also for American society at large. Nineteen sixty-five was either the pivotal year for spirituality and religion in America or perhaps just the symbolically critical one. Whichever way one may choose to see the matter, the fact remains that for the thirty years since, from the dawning of the Age of Aquarius and the crooning of the flower children to the present moment, the introduction of the sacred into everyday conversation and ordinary considerations has been a steady, documentable, direct evolution.

In April 1993 Wade Clark Roof, J. F. Rowny professor of religion and society at the University of California at Santa Barbara, published a book called *A Generation of Seekers: The Spiritual Journeys of the Baby Boom Generation* that quantitatively and qualitatively documents the foment of spirituality and religion in contemporary America among those adults most shaped by the sixties and their sequelae. By studying subjects' habits, practices, and self-assessments of values and goals, and repeated same-subject interviews, Roof was able to give faces and descriptive categorizations to the men and women who are that foment. At the same time he also furnished students of the sacred in America with that other standard of credible measure — descriptive demographics of overt and/or claimed behavior.

Roof's work was and remains seminal, so seminal in fact that its panoramic view of what is happening has come to be known as the Roof Report, while the report's title, *A Generation of Seekers,* has become the label of choice for characterizing contemporary adult America.[12] But how did we come to be susceptible to that kind of label? How did we who are adults in America today come to be either Roof's generation of seekers or else the parental source behind it? As Shakespeare once said, "Therein lieth the tale," or at least its beginning.

*　*　*　*　*

If distance and a sense of homesick separation from one's origins are conducive to questing for the sacred, then we late-twentieth-century Americans certainly have adequate justification for our present, immense absorption with it. Depending on who's doing the counting, some dozen to two dozen separate events, discoveries, and circumstances have contrived within the last hundred years to bombard western, and most particularly American, civilization in so dramatic a way as to sever us, its citizen-members, from all our past sureties. The last time such a wrenching happened, history labeled the whole thing the Renaissance or, in plain English, the "Rebirth"; and as more than one of my religionist friends has quipped recently, "Pray God we should all come out of this one half so blessed!" My own personal wager is heavily on the side of full beneficence, but more of that later. For the moment, there is a prior and demanding question that must be considered: What exactly is our circumstance in history in the closing years of the twentieth century in America?

What, in other words, are those dozen to two dozen events that have wrenched us loose from our moorings and, in the course of doing so, have redefined not only us but also the sea on which we sail? And second, how and where and by what taxonomy of definitions are you and I seeking to discover the sacred within the confines of our fixed circumstance? Answering these questions, it seems to me, is preliminary to any helpful discussion, even one based on so objective a thing as books, of spirituality and religion in an American context. And answering them is most certainly a first step toward exposing the nostalgia with which most of us as Americans address and define the sacred.

* * * * *

Almost anyone with half an ounce of social sensibility knows that in Hiroshima and its mushroom cloud the twentieth century found its axial event. After August 6, 1945, nothing was ever again to be as it had been. The political, moral, cultural, and humanitarian consequences of that first nuclear destruction are still being tallied. Paradoxically enough (or perhaps perversely enough), its impact on humanity's sense of the sacred was almost immediately perceivable.

On August 5 and on all the days of time prior to August 5 cataclysmic destruction had rested in the hands of the gods — the god of the storm, the god of the fire, the avenging god, the inscrutable but trustworthy god, and so forth — and there was patent in this theogenesis some point or directedness to our destruction, a patency that from the beginnings of memory had made massive death both conscionable and endurable. But on August 6, destruction was restructured as annihilation, and its uses moved into human hands. Destruction became potentially random and therefore pointless, and if pointless, then by default godless. It became absurd; and we became absurdists under the great mushroom cloud.

The rift between God and what mattered, between theology and spirituality within the construct of the sacred, had begun. It had begun big time, in fact; maybe not in our conscious thinking just yet and certainly not so immediately in our everyday American conversations, but it had begun. Only the Jews, coming out of the hideousness of their own cataclysm, survived 1945 with God and the sacred still sharing a common space. That difference between Jewish and a more general perception of annihilation was to become one of the informing differences in late-twentieth-century approaches to the sacred.

The majority of Americans in 1945, as is still true in the mid-nineties, were not Jews, however. Theirs was a goy perception uncushioned by a seamless orthodoxy. And to most of us born into that non-Jewish majority, what was good post-Hiroshima was life itself. Gradually but relentlessly, what we perceived as good (as opposed to what tradition had trained us to reverence as good) became the basis for how we empersoned the sacred. "The force which through the green fuse drives the flower drives my young life," Dylan Thomas had written in 1939. Within ten years, most Americans understood those words, heralding them as prophetic and Thomas himself as a prophet. Neither assessment has changed much in the fifty years since.

*   *   *   *   *

Just as Hiroshima's crucial influence on our times is obvious to everyone who cares to look, so too is Vietnam's. Vietnam had many repercussions. Most of them did not overtly have much to do with our sense of the sacred. One of them did. The one clear lesson that we as a citizenry got out of Vietnam was pervasive as well as central: Never trust authority — not its morals or its integrity or (God help us) its edicts, directions, and explanations. (The Civil Rights movement, a few assassinations, and Watergate were to further reenforce that basic lesson.) No authority, ever. Period. After Nam, Nixon, and that string of assassinations at home and abroad, the individual's perception of right and wrong, do and don't do, believe and don't believe became the litmus test for commitment and, interestingly enough, also for moral responsibility and judgment.

By their very nature, individual perceptions and institutional perceptions are naggingly at loggerheads even in the best of times. When, as happened during the sixties, the tension between internal and external authority becomes an intolerable and irresolvable conflict, however, individuals and groups of like-minded individuals eventually have to come down on one side or the other. America's baby boomers (born from 1946 to 1964 and about 80 million strong in America today),[13] who were the generation caught in this particular window of choice, came down firmly upon the side of internal authority. That decision has made all the difference, especially in their views of the sacred and even more especially in their views of how the sacred must be engaged. In other words, because they as baby boomers were/are many more in number, greater in influence, and more enfranchised financially than any other segment of late-twentieth-century America, their distrust of external authority[14] has made all the difference in contemporary America's attitudes toward the sacred and all things depending from it — morality, spirituality, faith, theology, and most assuredly, religion itself.

As a point midway in all of this foment, and because it serves nicely as a piece of convenient shorthand for an otherwise unruly complexity, 1965 is indeed usually cited, by untrained social commentators as well as by trained professionals like Barbara DeConcini, as the axial year for this second significant shift in American subjectivity.[15] It is almost exclusively the professional historians, however, and not the journalists or dilettante parade watchers, who are inclined to cite the closing of the American frontier as the third most influential event in the shaping of our contemporary American mind-set about the sacred.

*   *   *   *   *

We Americans have from the beginning been a geographically restive lot. There was always that frontier in front of us, winking at us from just beyond the right here and now. There was always the safety valve of its adventure to be dreamed of, if not actually pursued; and there was always — most blessed gift of all — its open possibility of escape from intolerable strictures. A man could be a man on the frontier, whatever that meant. (As it turns out, we are discovering that it meant a lot.)

Gradually during the first half of our century, the frontier slipped away, driven at last over the rim of California's far shore and into the sea. There was no farther place to run to, to dream of, to test ourselves against, or to exile our malefactors to; and there was no boundless supply of natural wealth. President Kennedy's space program, intended by him and Arthur Schlesinger Jr. as the new frontier, gave us only Camelot, and that far too briefly. In the end, we had to accept ourselves as confined, effectively speaking, to planet Earth and to each other.

So the discovery that the frontier was forever gone was for most midcentury adult Americans a startling one, destined to impact their, and subsequently our, sense of Earth herself as much as our self-image of all Americans as potential John and Jane Waynes, that is, as hearty but god-chosen and god-blessed individualists freed by expanse and opportunity from the restraints of too much mutuality.

The discovery of a frontier that had dwindled away more than snapped shut was also disorienting. When a man or woman has walked hunched into the wind all of his or her life and when the wind then abruptly drops and is still, that man or woman drops too — face down and in the mud, usually. What our pioneering and wind-facing grandparents had sought from the sacred, in other words, suddenly became as useless and apparently inappropriate to us, their frontierless children, as a sailor's call for fancier riggings would seem in a becalmed sea.

After Camelot, challenge was dead — unavoidable, life-engendering physical challenge, that is — and with it went the excitement and validation of physical accomplishment. With it went also a whole tradition of American spiritual practice, the tradition of generations and generations of petitioners who engaged the sacred only theologically and only as supplicants. And nobody, not even a professional historian, can overemphasize the consequences of that shift, for into the vacuum of lost sensation and lost engagement slipped what the world at large so fondly referred to for three envious decades as "the American lifestyle" and what we all more wisely and cynically now refer to as "blatant consumerism."

Made possible by the bitterly won technologies of a world war, that lifestyle filled our American mid- and latter-midcentury with — what else? — sensation. On that much we can all agree. When exactly sensation slipped over into being excessive gratification is a little less clear, but slip it did. And with it went our attention, the shifting of our focus from our centers to our perimeters where the action was — where the neon and the chrome were, the cars and the music and the foolheartedness of stocking twenty-seven different brands of canned english peas in every supermarket. Too much. We knew we were drowning ourselves in too much. Minimalism became a defining hallmark of the sacred, a necessary elegance within it. Sensing this, we needed only the rhetoric, the traditions, and the disciplines of simplicity explained in order to clasp simplicity to ourselves as healing for the new ache of consciousness' displacement.

As chance or design would have it, three wars — World War II, Korea, and Vietnam (wars that had cost the world so much) — were also to save us. They had scattered Americans widely across Asia and thereby broadcast them about in lands and cultures where simplicity is a studied discipline of the soul in quest of itself. Concepts of mindfulness and intricacy that would have been alien to earlier Americans were by 1975, if not familiar, at least less inaccessible than they once had been. In many American homes and communities, such precepts were in fact resident for the first time. Buddhism, Zen, Taoism, and Shintoism, the worldviews most centrally built on the principles of transcendent spiritual discipline as a means of entering and engaging the sacred, had for the first time in our history taken up a place among us, not only because of the culturally enhanced experiences of our returning young soldiers but also, and far more portentously, because of the rich, almost innate spirituality of their war brides and their bicultural children.

*   *   *   *   *

In addition to the three megaexperiences of Hiroshima, Vietnam, and the lost frontier, there have been in the decades since the Great Depression several other formative occurrences. Less frequently discussed, these social changes have had subjective consequences for the present time. And if we are to set our search for the sacred properly within its contemporary context, at least three of these seem to me to require our detailed attention.

Just as the impact of Hiroshima and Vietnam and a closing frontier upon Americans' interior life has been appreciably different in its expression from the impact of those same events upon our external activities, so too has the impact of drugs been very, very different within each of those two spheres. Drugs have shaped and colored irreversibly our late-twentieth-century knowledge of the subjective world and our understanding of its constituencies, including our understanding of the sacred. To deny either that fact or its painfully earned bank of resulting information would be as foolhardy as it is almost willfully naive. That is, drug use — both rampant, destructive, illegal, abusive use and controlled, social, religious, licensed use — has told us a great deal about what is psychological as well as bio- and neurochemical. In so doing, it may have told us even more about what is sacred. Drug use has certainly forced us to think a great deal about the distinctions that must be made among them.

Some of our thinking about that issue, in the last thirty years, has also been based on laboratory-controlled studies, investigations that have resulted in, and come out of, the newer sciences of neurobiology or neurochemistry, neurochemical medicine and neurosurgery. By the end of the great Renaissance, Descartes had been able to conclude, *Cognito, ergo sum* [I think, therefore I am]. And most of western culture, especially at the popular level, has used that thesis for four hundred years as a kind of ultimate security blanket. But when consciousness can be altered and behavior changed, whether chemically or mechanically, in consistent and predictable ways, who exists?

Who is it that "is"? That was, and remains, a stunning question, all the more so because it has intruded upon every level of American life from the Prozac patient to the kid on the corner rather than just upon the informed life of some cloistered philosopher or white-coated laboratory scientist. But because as a question it has intruded so violently into both the experience and the ordinary information sources of workaday folk, it has, unlike most of history's previous "big" questions, intruded upon those of us who are singularly ill-prepared by tradition or education to address such an existential and essential quandary. Certainly in the 1960s and 1970s, when the drug culture first inundated the culture at large, we were a society almost totally without coping mechanisms and absolutely without an appropriate education. Quite literally, we hadn't educed it yet, nor have we still.

Right from the beginning, the central questions of consciousness were unsettling ones for thousands of Americans. But for many of our young, thoughtful, and restless in those early days of the New Age the questions, when followed for very long, tended to point straight into the door of the nearest ashram or to a sweat lodge or to a cloister like Thomas Merton's Gethsemani. Following the questions of consciousness, in other words, tends to point us to those places and those human communities where such questions have been resident for more centuries than here and where the answers have already been polished by use and domesticated by affection. The significant — perhaps one could even dare to say the saving — detail is, of course, that such sanctuaries are all schoolhouses of the spirit, not the intellect; and their consoling information is spiritual rather than theological.

To this generalized mix of drug-born information, controlled experimentation, and roiling confusion we have added, like mischievous jinns to a tableau, the work of Freud and Jung, of Joseph Campbell and, as popularizers, of Bill Moyers and Jean Houston. The result has been astonishing. In a matter of less than three decades, the average American has gained a whole new geography — the universal unconscious. With its archetypes and its staggering cross-cultural similarities, its parallels and fixed accoutrements, the universal unconscious was the hidden continent we all had known was there but never dared acknowledge out loud before. It became our new frontier. And the relationship of this new terrain to the sacred, the spiritual, and the divine, for even the most unskilled explorer (clearly the three were at the very least different continents in the subjective cosmos), was as lost in our benighted ignorance as that between North America and India in the geographic naiveté of Christopher Columbus.

In addition to all of these effects of drug use and psycho/drug information upon our yearning for a conceivable sacred, there has been a third, and rather ironic, concomitant occurrence. One of the parts of the human experience that from the beginning has wedded the sacred to the theological is catastrophic illness. Like war before Hiroshima, illness before the 1940s seemed to rest in the hands of a cajolable god; and placating that god was a full-time preoccupation in a disease-filled, danger-filled world. Not only were supplication and sacrifice necessary to cure illness, but moral adherence to religious law was necessary to prevent it.

There is absolutely no reason to assume, of course, that both these principles of cure and prevention are not just as operative today as they ever were. The point is that they certainly did fall from grace in the American popular mind during the sixties, seventies, and eighties. Looking back now, of course, most of us would say that the illnesses we learned to cure and/or prevent in those halcyon days were only replaced by new and more terrible ones.

We suspect, in other words, that we have replaced our grandparents' horror of pneumonia with our own anguish over AIDS, and their anxiety over the scourge of smallpox with ours over cancer — which is neither to say nor to imply that a cause-and-effect relationship existed, but simply to acknowledge that humanity seems foreordained to vulnerability by whatever name and that precious few of us grasped that fact very quickly. Instead, during our midcentury years, as the nineteenth century work of Lister and Pasteur began to eventuate in effective antibacterial procedures and as sulfa drugs and penicillin began to perform their effective but nonshamanistic sleight of hand, we felt safe, however falsely, for the first time in history.

The fact that many of us have now returned, or do return, to our knees when faced with illness is not as significant to the question of the sacred, however, as is what we learned during our brief period of imagined impunity. Thinking ourselves invulnerable at last, we thumbed our noses at the whole theory of an intervening God and went looking for fun without him. In a sense, what we did, not so much individually as aggregately, was swap theology for psychiatry.

The hiatus in our perceived need for praying and the interruption of our dependency on clergy of one sort or another turned out to be productive, if expensive, side trips. They freed the sacred, however wrenchingly, of its ordained gatekeepers. They opened the land of the interior to unguided and unfettered exploration by ordinary travelers and even by a few weekend picnickers.[16] In doing so, of course, these forays also exposed us as a society to epidemic proportions of some very terrible agonies of body, soul, mind, and spirit.

There is no question, for instance, that circumstances in the last half of this century have forced us as a nation and as individuals to shift our attention, fiscally as well as politically, from threats like tuberculosis to horrors like endemic depression and pervasive social violence. One of the sequelae of such debilitating ills, aside from the obvious ones, is that, when considered nontheologically, they can seem at first blush to be the result of human malfunction and therefore subject to human correction. They can when so assessed engender an inordinate amount of human guilt and produce an equally disproportionate amount of human frustration. Yet those very difficulties have forced many of us to travel, for ourselves and in our own way, even deeper into the no-longer-patroled interior; and both the experiences of increased, social distress and individualized journeying have helped clarify for just plain, average people the differences between the sacred and the phenomenology of our own embodied minds.

*   *   *   *   *

To say that only one more piece of twentieth-century history warrants detailed discussion in this overview of what has led to our current American absorption with the sacred is certainly not to say that there are no others to discuss. There are. Not only do other causes and reasons exist, but some of them are routinely given more prominence of place than are one or two of the factors I have chosen to emphasize here.

For example, the whole phenomenon of mass communication, massive immigration, and our resulting awareness of a global village has eroded old ways and introduced even older ones like the home as workplace, tribalism, a zealous almost pathologic absorption with observing over participating, and the like. Most especially is this true here in America, where "old," at least Eurocentrically speaking, is anything that happened twenty-five years ago.

The impact of television is incalculable in every part and parcel of human experience. No piece of ourselves has been more subtly and painfully shaped by television's cold-medium effects, however, than has our emotional life. The yearning to feel again has become almost a phrenetic agony for many Americans and has directly governed what we see as, and seek from, the sacred.

Urbanization in general and the move by middle America from a goods-based to a money-based life in particular have deeply wounded us, severing as they have our selves from our own abilities and needs, as well as our being from our doing. The coming in the late nineteenth century of Theosophy as a movement among our intellectuals,[17] of Vivekananda as the first guru to achieve popular visibility and audience in North America, of the first Parliament of the World's Religions to Chicago — these are often cited as additional explanations of just why and how the twentieth century could adapt so smoothly to eastern philosophies and spiritual disciples in the decades after our three Far Eastern conflicts.

Certainly, and perhaps most important in terms of its consequences for our discovering of the sacred, the disestablishment of authority in the culture at large led even more directly than did the consequences of technology to the disparagement of the clergy in America, as I have already said. But this withdrawal from belief in, and dependence upon, the ordained of whatever faith was tragically reenforced in the popular mind by the scandals of the televangelists of the eighties, the exposed faith healers of every decade, and, of course, most recently the clerical and priestly sexual abuses of the nineties. Public distrust, in other words, has of late become public disgust — a bitter shift. The most reportable result, at least quantitatively, has been that established religion and most particularly mainline, established clergy have been rendered almost impotent pastorally, unable either to attract or to counsel the spiritual seeker skittish of their track record and the possible high cost of their advice.

This list of causes and consequences could undoubtedly go meaningfully on to include several other, equally formative entries, but ultimately any list must also be true to its maker, signatory inevitably of the patterns and causes of its author. For that reason and because I am a product of the Great Depression who has lived through the bulk of this century as well as read about it, I have chosen instead to emphasize only one other, last piece of modernity, one that I see as perhaps the most far-ranging of them all. Though she is not often elaborated upon by other professional analysts of the sacred in American life, I think she is unavoidable in any realistic discussion of it. So I bring you one last explanatory idea for how I think we got to be a nation of questers. I bring you Rosie the riveter.

*   *   *   *   *

Whatever else she did during World War II, Rosie, the Riveter about whom our mid-century sang and made jokes as well as movies, changed America just as surely as she saved it; and while hers may not be the most elegant explanation of sacredness in our closing years of this millennium, it is still probably one of the more pivotal ones, at least on the bedrock level of individual and private lives. Rosie went to work during World War II making planes and guns and tanks to keep her man safe while he made the world safe for her and their babies; and as a nation America praised her in proportion to how desperately it needed her to wield her riveting gun.

Rosie had stood beside her man before, of course, battling right alongside him in the fields against drought and insects, in the winter against starvation and cold, in the sickroom against malevolent fate, in the kitchen and garden and storeroom against want, and in the marketplace of domestic productivity against a cashless life. But Rosie had done all those things *beside* her man. Now he was a world away and she, like some kind of bandanna-turbaned Molly Pitcher, was alone and doing it. By God and to her own amazement, she was doing it!

How much Rosie's paycheck changed her definition of gratification is still under discussion; but there is no question that that check gave her freedom, nor was there any question that Rosie's freedom, while it was only economic and psychological in 1945 when Johnny came marching home again, had forever redefined Rosie. *Beside* wasn't nearly so attractive anymore. More to the point, *beside* wasn't even necessary anymore.

Johnny, on the other hand, was war-weary and totally innocent of Rosie's private evolution during the years of their separation. In Johnny's mind, the years had been ones in which Rosie's life had been fixed, changeless, in a kind of suspended animation. The conflict that resulted between the sexes over that difference (i.e., between her actuality and his arrested perception) was, as we now know, worked out more domestically than politically in those first few years of change. But it simmered, waiting until 1961 and The Pill. Now the shift in gender roles became political, because now Rosie was biologically free as well.

The consequences of economic empowerment, biological control, and psychological enfranchisement for Rosie sent America spinning in a maelstrom of change that is still thundering. The abortion issue became the principal forum for the public arguing of woman's rights and place, but the nuclear family became the site for its decisive skirmishes. How much contemporary blame one chooses or refuses to assign to Rosie, her riveting machine, and her pill is a matter of private responsibility. However innocent or guilty Rosie may have been of her own consequences, though, the fact still remains that no longer was the family the holding center in most American lives. As that center slipped and as Rosie's bandanna changed slowly into pantyhose and a three-piece Hunter's Ridge business suit, so too did our sense of the sacred begin to pick up its first hint of the nostalgic. The sacred, we knew in our remembering hearts, had once been resident — surely must still be resident — in the ordinary, the domestic, the shared table, the homemade and the handmade.

Part of all of this was the fact that after Rosie's war the American family began to move. Whether or not this was partly due to Rosie's restlessness is unimportant. The informing thing is that the family moved and that, therefore, when it broke up or hit troubled waters, it and all its members lacked the anchor of proximate, extended family. It was as if not only the altar stones but the whole sacred grove were gone.

All the pressures to conform to a given code, all the stories that distilled family honor and reenforced community standards, all the comfort of continuity, all the cohesion of working as a unit or group for the benefit of the whole, all the perspective of deeply intimate shared experience, all the sanctuary of endurance that had prevailed, and all the blessedness of earth and natal place were gone, gone half a world away or half a continent, half a state or half a county, but gone. Rosie and Johnny were rudderless in America, and their children? Let's face it. The working majority of us today are their children or their children's children.

– 3 –

What We Believe In

ROSIE AND JOHNNY did their work well. Their children and grandchildren are now America's over-thirties and number 160 million strong. In a nation of approximately 255 million, we constitute almost three-fifths of the population and are the most enabled, enfranchised generation[1] in American history.

But for all the talk about our being seekers, the baldfaced truth is that, first and foremost, we are believers. A stereotype-shattering 93 percent of us told pollsters in 1994 that we believe in God or a universal spirit.[2] Studies of the religious practices by which we give observable expression to that kind of widely broadcast belief are, as we have already noted, a bit easier to conduct and a good deal more objective; and there certainly has been no lack of them over the past three or four years either. Depending on which study one cites, somewhere between 70 and 80 million of us claim to be active (i.e., attend church at least once a month) Christians and approximately 6 out of every 10 of us attend either synagogue, mosque, or church regularly.

Perhaps even more telling of our believer status is what we are publicly willing to admit to privately doing, even to that most violate of questioners, the media. Nine out of ten Americans, for example, recently told *Life* that they "pray frequently and earnestly."[3] Fifty-one percent of us who do pray said that we pray once or twice a day; but an additional 24 percent of us pray three or more times each day, 28 percent of us for more than an hour.

And 95 percent of all of us *know* that our prayers have, at one time or another, been answered.

A nation of seekers, certainly. The evidence for that is irrefutable statistically (and for most of us experientially, which is by far the more persuasive of the two.) But before we are seekers, we first are believers; and those beliefs determine — almost confine, in fact — what we seek and how. And interestingly enough, if the books we buy and the materials we choose to spend our free time with are true indicators, our over-thirty beliefs are much nearer to early humanity's than Rosie's and Johnny's were. We have apparently gone full circle, as it were, only to arrive at a kind of neoprimalism,[4] albeit a remarkably orthodox one.

*   *   *   *   *

Even a cursory study of the lists of successful sacral/spiritual/religious books published over the last three or four years exposes four general groups into which the bulk of them can be sorted and placed, four large categories of like-minded or interconnected materials that, for lack of any better term, I have come to call "belief constructs." There are, in other words, certain subcategories of books about our subjective experiences, needs, and interests that seem to me to lump themselves together into one of four larger categories on the basis of their having a subterranean but shared set of suppositions. (There are a few smaller, but presently less influential, such groups as well.)

We over-thirties, when we read books[5] and especially when we read books about spiritual, sacred, or religious matters, have for the last two or three years selected a book from the stack of volumes about near-death experiences more frequently than from any other subtype.[6]

We believe,

or we want to believe,

or we seek justification for believing,

or we seek relief...

...the relief (and this seems to be the case for a surprising and growing number of us) of knowing that someone else has also had such a life-changing experience, and the consolation as well of sharing through a book the pain, surprise, and often bitter joy of that experience's repercussions.

But regardless of which or how many of those reasons for reading a book about near-death experiences may be operative with any given reader at any given time, the point is that we believe, want to believe, or believe that we actually already *know* from personal experience, something about be-ing beyond human death.

The business of conceptualizing ourselves beyond bodily death is hardly a new enterprise. It has been the moral carrot as well as the consolation blanket of most theistic societies from the very start of recorded time. What is new, at least in United States times, is belief in a tunnel or passageway into a light of great benignity, personness, and ajudgmental acceptance. Such envisioning speaks geographically of another realm of being that, once passed into, is, and is as life is, not as place or mind is. Such a belief is essentially useless as a whipping stick for sectarianism or fixed doctrines, but it is a powerful motivator toward goodness as charity defines that trait. It is also, and somewhat paradoxically, both consoling (who among us does not want to know that this life's difficulties and tragedies are only temporary and precursory?) and frightening (who among us wants to fall helpless into such transmogrification?) So we read.

And what we read about second in this broad category is angels. They are only agents of the light and therefore safer as well as closer to us. They also, blessedly, have bodies and can even assume ones like our own or like those of other earthly creatures who also presently live by means of bodies. Angels, while they may not experience human life as such, can at least perceive its problems and interfere in the course of things by changing occurrences to our benefit. Angels, moreover, act in two states — the one on this side of the separating tunnel and the one on the far side of that passage.

Their comings and goings attest to the semipermeableness of that membrane between us and the Other. Security in this realm of experience; proofs of another. Why, for goodness' sake, wouldn't we want to know more about angels? And knowing, why wouldn't we believe ever more assuredly in a realm beyond our sight that is filled with beings as well as Be-ing?

And if angels, then why not other orders as well, or at the very least, orders of angels? of saints? of bodhisattvas? of...? Well, why not? And if these, then why not also channeling and inspiration and prophecy, for we read those books[7] in unbelievable quantities.

And if there are those who channel[8] to us and those who, in their mercy, intercede for us, how can we really know that all of them are from beyond the tunnel? Indeed we cannot, nor do most of us even pretend to try to believe that all life is beyond it. Such a limitation confounds the imagination and therefore our belief. Some Other life, presently unseen but corporeal as ours is, surely must also exist within this experience. Sheer odds, at least popularly speaking, say that there must be other inhabited worlds striving to reach us as well as a few that are even managing to engage us.

"E.T., phone home" may not, at first glance, seem to be a matter of the sacred so much as of the sciences. On second and subsequent glances, however, aliens and our modern involvement with them are very much a part of the present sacred/religious/spiritual mix. Theologically, the possibility of aliens' existence bombards almost every doctrinal system in this world. Subjectively, the concept of aliens as powerful friends introduces angel-like agents of humanoid rather than divine nature.[9] Intellectually, the study of altered states of consciousness, including work on subjects with alien experiences, requires even greater delving into the basic definitions of humanness as well as of the relation between it and the whole of which it is but one part.[10]

Whether one believes personally in all or any part of the scenarios I have just outlined is essentially unimportant to our present discussion; the important thing is that we as a group function somewhere between belief in and curiosity about such possibilities. The point, in other words, really is that as seekers we are also conceptualizers, and what we have conceptualized and what we reference out from as well as back to is a multirealmed existence and a multi-inhabited one in which we are less powerful, but in aggregate more significant, every day. There is something out there and beyond here and all around there and here that wants us, something that knows us, something that seeks us. . . .

That is what I mean by a belief construct. It is also the first of my four such groupings. The second is subtler, but like the serpent, more beautiful: We think we have lost something and that what we have lost was, once upon a former time, well-known to us and can, if we look hard enough, be rediscovered and repossessed.

The presence in our lives, more or less nontheistically, of many multiple realms and multiple orders of creatures is part of what I mean when I speak of "neoprimalism." Whether my term is adequate or not, the proof of what it's trying to define lies just as much in mythic agents and multiple worlds as in this contemporary sense of our dislocation from, well, from wisdom. We don't seem to have a better word for that one either, unless we capitalize it into "Wisdom" or qualify it — which is exactly what we more frequently do — into "ancient" or "timeless" wisdom.

＊　＊　＊　＊　＊

The second area presently of interest to American readers of books about the religious, the sacred, and the spiritual is also the largest single grouping of them; that is, the total number of individual, commercially successful titles in this category is greater than in any other, but there are also fewer megaselling superstars within it. I refer, of course, to books of ancient wisdom.[11]

As a principle, a sense of dislocation — of something deeply integral having been lost — is a focused one. The means sought for remedying that fracture, however, are diffuse; and which one a seeker chooses seems to depend to a large extent on the frame of reference out of which he or she comes. Thus, Karen Armstrong's *A History of God,* when it hit the charts in late 1993 and early 1994, did so presumably because monotheists and would-be monotheists wanted to know the beginnings of what they were personally involved with. There simply is not any other very probable explanation for *History*'s astonishing commercial success.

By the same token, among the monotheists in America's over-thirties the huge majority are Christian; and our frames of reference have pushed onto the charts books about Christianity's lost, or at least misplaced, beginnings. Books like the Jesus Seminar's *The Five Gospels,* Dom Crossan's *The Historical Jesus,* Bishop Jack Spong's *Born of a Woman* or *Resurrection — Myth or Reality?* and the like — all hit the bestseller lists for extended periods and all are now consistent sellers in paperback editions as well. All of them also are part of the so-called search for the historical Jesus, by which we mean the attempt to pry off from the God/man of Nazareth all the editorializing and elaborations and politicking modifications of time, religious enthusiasm, and institutional self-interest in order to arrive back at what *really* was, the assumption clearly being that what we now have is less than, as well as far more suspect than, that presupposed original.[12] In much the same spirit and apparently driven by the same hungers, almost any book about the Dead Sea Scrolls, the ancient texts found in the library of the Essene community at Qum'ran in 1947, or about the Gnostic texts found at Nag Hammadi in Egypt in 1945 both sell and maintain themselves as well, through long shelf lives.

The search for knowledge as a divine agent or as a tool for getting at the divine is itself gnostic, after the Greek word *gnosis,* meaning "knowledge"; and Gnosticism with a capital *G* was one of the earliest rivals of, and finally heresies within, Christianity. The Gospel of Thomas, the fifth Gospel in *The Five Gospels,*[13] is a

Gnostic text. That does not mean that Thomas's gospel is any less or any more authentic; it simply means that we care less about the possibility of heresy than we do about the possibility that knowing what *Thomas* says may help us ascertain what *really* was said. And suddenly, of course, we are right back to speaking from the same perspective of truth once known and later lost.

* * * * *

Christians, in their yearning, believing search for the historical or real Jesus, have reached out, almost by default, to his Jewishness and their own religious origins within Judaism. The result has been literally dozens of books since 1993 on "Jesus the Jew," "Yesh'va for our times," "rediscovering Christianity's Hebrew roots," and the like. My labels are generic, but the phenomenon is very specific. In addition to this Semitization of Christianity[14] has come an expansion of public awareness about the Holocaust and of our national anguish over it. As a subcategory, books on the Holocaust have increased Christian awareness of the Jewish experience sympathetically. Moreover, so much focus on the history and condition of the Jewish people and upon their endurance in the face of such unspeakable adversity has also led many Christians to ask whether some part of the missing wholeness in their own lives might not just still be locateable within Orthodox, or historical, Judaism itself. Books for Christians about Jewish holy days and mysticism, in particular, have proliferated — books for Christians, not (or not just) for Jews, that is.

Christians, because they are divisible into thousands[15] of doctrinally distinct groups, differ in their definitions of what is, with reference to their faith, "ancient." Roman Catholic and liturgical Christians can, however, lay honest claim to having been the first institutionalized expression of Christianity as well as to being, with 60 million–plus members, the largest single body of Christians in America today. Even so, nobody, bookseller or otherwise, was prepared for the instantaneous skyrocketing of sales[16] for the new Catechism of the Roman Church when it was released in July 1994. A book that was originally perceived as a user's manual for priests and bishops responsible for the operation and beliefs of the church, in actuality became a personal necessity for lay men and women who (Is this beginning to sound as familiar as the chorus of a good drinking song?) wanted "to know what the church *really* teaches" and/or, but far more titillating as a reason for buying a rather ponderous book, "to find out what the church was really like before it got all Americanized." The quotes again are my own wording, but they represent accurately the explanations I have heard dozens of times over, both from booksellers quoting their customers and from the customers themselves.

In addition to the supernovas of the Catechism and Pope John Paul II's *Crossing the Threshold of Hope* (1994), yearning for the timeless wisdom of liturgical Christianity's beginnings has led to dozens of new books over the past five years or so about the early church fathers and on Saint Augustine in particular, as well as to the reissue of many of the classics of Roman Catholicism. In this latter endeavor, the reissue specifically for the over-thirties lay audience of the classics of the faith has even spawned a few publishing houses. Of these newcomers the Sophia Institute Press is among the more successful.[17] And I can't help wondering if its name were not an invocation to at least some of its good fortune: *sophia* is the Greek word for — what else? — wisdom; when capitalized into *Sophia,* it is the proper name as well for that emanation of God celebrated in the Old Testament as his Holy Spirit, his handmaiden and his counselor.

The other largest congress of Christians in this country is a loose confederation of many denominations and fellowships that all regard themselves as Evangelicals. Because they are Protestant doctrinally, their sense of proprietary wisdom retreats only as far back as the Reformation and Enlightenment thinkers, but here too the same phenomenon of dislocation and powerfully motivated searching has occurred. In many ways the religio-political Right is an expression of this sense of the need to return and relocate something once had and now lost. Certainly the books of the so-called religious Right, if looked at dispassionately, reflect much of this kind of yearning. Even the development over the last twenty years of a strong Evangelical publishing industry in this country may itself be said to be in no small part a result of this very need to reach back and connect.[18]

The proliferation of Jewish-imprint publishing and — very marked by within the last year or two — the increase in number of titles about "reclaiming historic Judaism" as a lived faith further attests to this same mind-set in America's second-largest faith system. Where assimilation had been the order of the day in our midcentury, the return to "old ways" is now the emphasis. Books about "old ways," however, don't derive just from mainstream Orthodox Judaism but increasingly include medieval, mystical, Kabalistic, and Hasidic themes as well.[19]

* * * * *

For many of us — one is tempted almost to say for all of us, so widespread is the phenomenon — the ancient truths of our inherited landmass are tantalizing regardless of, and in concert with, our individual birth traditions. Somehow those Native Americans who preceded most of us here *knew* something we no longer do or else never did — something about how to respect the earth as mother, to be reverent before the mystery of life, to walk in balance with all life, and to speak sagely rather than factually. The books about Native American spirituality (which was among the first of the non-Christian spiritualities to achieve popular acceptance)[20] began to come out in some quantity in the late eighties; and since the success of Leslie Silko's *Ceremony* and *The Almanac of the Dead*, there has been no letup in sight.

Books about the Native American spiritual experience are closely related to books researching and presenting the spiritual experience of every other group of seekers among us from that of the displaced African American to Robert Bly's demythologized *Iron John*. Aboriginal and primitive religions have never before received such attention in book, or any other, form as they have since Joseph Campbell first perceived our need and began to try to satisfy it. Likewise, talk of the primitive, because it contains talk of the feminine, has found expression in books ranging from volumes on wicca to ones on feminist theology.

While many critics of this kind of free-ranging ecumenism in our over-thirties see such books as cutting too close to magic and incantational hocus-pocus, public absorption will out; it continues to drive the publishing engine, being especially insistent in those areas of ancient wisdom that embrace or are contiguous to the feminine. A longing for gender stability in the culture at large and a universally human longing for intimate nurture have lent the area additional emotional urgency; and all kinds of gender-issue subgroups, the majority of them feminist, have thrived as a result within the broad area of sacral/religious/spirituality publishing. Ecology; Marianism; religious biographies of female figures as diverse as David Epstein's *Sister Aimee* and, in her own way, the royal J. of Harold Bloom and David Rosenburg's *The Book of "J"*; nostalgic books about domestic experience, marriage, the sanctity of the ordinary — there are many modern faces to the ancient goddess.

While no one, least of all me, wants to become tedious by protracting a proof list well beyond the need for further examples, one more presentation of our American belief in ancient wisdom — its existence, its efficacy, our severance from it — just must be mentioned. There is in the adult population at large in this country a positive mushrooming of interest in Buddhism. This too has dramatically impacted the book industry. In addition to an expansion in their Buddhism publishing program by well-known, older houses like Beacon, HarperSanFrancisco, Shambhala, Chas. Tuttle, and the like, we have also had within the last six or seven years the establishment of Buddhist-only outlets like Snow Lion or

Parallax Publishing for books or *Tricycle* magazine in periodicals, all of them enjoying brisk sales and serving growing audiences.[21]

The fascinating thing about the growth of Buddhism in this country[22] is that Buddhism is itself a wisdom system; that is, Buddhism is not strictly speaking a theistic faith but rather an understanding or realization. Because it is nontheistic, it offers no real impediment to those of other, theistic, backgrounds who wish to pursue its insights, meditative disciplines, and consolations. A Zen Buddhist Christian, in other words, is a perfectly possible, if somewhat adjectivally encumbered, construct. (Not only do I know a few of them personally, but at least seven or eight whom I don't know published books on the subject in 1994 alone.)

Because Buddhism is one of, if not the, fastest growing subarea of sacred/spiritual/religious publishing in America today and because we must assume that that growth is reflective of emphases resident in the book-buying public itself, we can safely say of this second of our four belief constructs that whatever else it may have done for us, it certainly has added a touch of the exotic to our lives. Not only do we Americans believe in ancient wisdom as healing for our subjective needs, but apparently we believe as well that it may ultimately be found, in whole or in part, in eastern rather than western history.[23]

* * * * *

The third belief construct that informs our seeking today is also the oldest. By virtue of having a history of sorts, it requires the least elaboration and is certainly the most entertaining. It, quite literally, has been all over the social map in this country, supported by everything from celebrity participants to endorsements from mainstream religions. Just the incongruities among its proponents could easily be the stuff of another book.

As a phenomenon, self-help — which is the overt expression of my third belief construct — began with Alcoholics Anonymous (AA) and its Twelve Step program. From that position of inestimable success and benefit, the idea spread out to include, in one way or another, almost every form of subjective or bodily ill that had any social context or implications.

The movement, right from its AA beginnings, used books — first as basic tools and eventually as a way of expanding its range and depth of applications. The first evidence of a broad-based belief in self-help (and, we could add, of a public belief in the moral obligation to try self-help), however, appeared first in books from small, specialized, or underground book publishers, many of which saw themselves as so-called New Age houses. But during the late eighties, riding a wave of public demand, self-help entered the general book market rather dramatically, peaked there about 1992–93, and then began to level off to its present, very secure position with the reading public. Before that leveling had actually begun to settle into place, however, self-help books had also begun to be a significant part of the publishing program of denominational and religion-imprint houses as well, making it perhaps the only subject area within which all segments of America's book industry have ever participated simultaneously.

As a belief construct, the self-help movement is extremely significant for us as generations of seekers. Convinced of our dislocation from something of original importance that is nonetheless still attainable, we over-thirties have been taught by it to perceive our limitations as remediable — but only if we can find the right set of habits and attitudes by which to purge ourselves of the ills acquired through ignorance or cultural contamination or simply as a result of being human.

The original Twelve Steps of the program were religious, albeit generically religious rather than doctrinally specific; and all the adaptations of it have remained essentially so as well. The beneficial effectiveness of the AA/self-help movement, however, militates for a belief in our own ability to discover a regimen for change and reenforces us in accepting the aid of a generalized "other." It has also tilted our interest in spirituality toward its practical uses, in itself a substantive shift in paradigms. The result has been a veritable sea of books about everything from our physical bodies to our spiritual consciousness.

It is, in fact, out of the success of self-help and our belief in it that much of the present "spirituality movement" may be said to have come,[24] for much contemporary American spirituality is a re-costumed and refurbished form of self-help that seeks more the well-being of its subject than any contemplation of the sacred.[25] The truncations of this approach have not prevented it from finding solid and intriguing presentations in book form. There are, for example, over twenty-five hundred books in print about meditation, prayers, and techniques for spiritual growth. From M. Scott Peck's quintessential bestseller *The Road Less Traveled* to the healing works of Larry Dossey and Dr. Deepak Chopra to the almost equally immortal books of Richard Foster on spiritual formation, from manuals by the Dalai Lama and Thich Nhat Hanh to even, in a bizarre but documentable connection, the economic guides of sectarian writers like Larry Burkett with his *The Coming Economic Earthquake* — all are selling well; all are rooted in our present sacral/spiritual/religious search; and all share a common, underlying belief:

We believe that, if only we try hard enough, we can.

We are, in other words, presently separated by only a very little from the pioneering spirit that was Rosie's remembered heritage. To be less than self-helpers would be un-American; and to be un-American is somehow worse than to be graceless, especially in a heavily Protestant context. It produces, also, a belief construct — the only one of our four of which this may be said — that emotionally is much more American than primal.

*   *   *   *   *

The fourth grouping of books, based on their speaking to a common area of interest in the reading public, is fiction, a genre more than a category and as nonprescriptive in its being as self-help can be formulaic in its. Call it religious fiction or inspirational fiction or by any of its sectarian names of Jewish, Catholic, Christian, or Evangelical. Or call it by some combination of them, like religious mysteries, Jewish historical novels, Evangelical Christian westerns, inspirational romances, and so on. Call it by whatever descriptive marker may come to mind. It doesn't matter, so long as the chosen label distinguishes fiction that exists first to serve the sacred in one way or another from fiction that exists first to serve the art of the written word or the gods of the cash register.

The presence of so many possible shelving labels and display sections has confused and annoyed book readers and booksellers for the last seven or eight years as the genre has begun to blossom and the number of its subcategories to grow. This embarrassment of excess in terms exists because we have continued to regard them all as competing possibilities. In reality, I think, they are each individually specific to some one of the many subcategories that together form a greater whole. Believing that, I am going to go out on my own limb and say that the fourth and last category of the greatest interest today to readers of religion/spirituality/sacredness materials is that of faith fiction.

Purists may argue that such a category is hardly a new one. God knows — quite literally, God knows — they are correct. The Abrahamic faiths — Judaism, Christianity, Islam — are almost the sum of religious adherence in America today, and they are, all three of them, "people of the story." Although that phrase, like the Haggadah itself, is most often assigned in popular parlance to Judaism, the fictive heritage of Christianity and Islam likewise is integral to their respective faiths.

But at a practical level of contemporary, author-created story, faith fiction is a grouping that began to come into its own just within the last few years, if we mean by that a grouping that began to have authors with million-plus sales and proliferating but distinct subcategories of story types.[26]

In 1983 when Fr. Joseph Girzone had finished writing a story about an updated, modern-day Jesus dealing with contemporary problems, he had to throw up his own publishing house, Richelieu Court, in order to get it published. But that first *Joshua* novel now stands as one of the bestselling novels of this century. It also opened the eyes of our domestic book industry to the enormous potential in the faith fiction category.

Joshua's popularity quickly led to *Joshua and the Children, The Shepherd* (still a Joshua book), and *Joshua in the Holy Land*, except that by that stage of Father Girzone's highly visible literary career, Macmillan, one of the country's largest and most respected publishing houses, had become his publisher. Then in 1993 Doubleday, for a reported pittance of $6 million in advance, took over Macmillan's place as Father Girzone's publisher, contracting to reissue *Joshua* in gift edition and to publish his first commercial nonfiction work as well as the next Joshua tale, *Joshua in New York*.

While Father Girzone came to his storytelling out of the mindset and traditions of liturgical Christianity, Frank Peretti came to his from a Protestant and different perspective, that of Pentecostal Christianity. Peretti's, in other words, is a Third Wave, spiritual-warfare point of view not much in vogue among America's general interest booksellers and librarians. Fourteen publishers rejected *This Present Darkness* before an Evangelical Christian publisher, Crossway Books, took it on — took it on, managed to sell 2 million copies of it, and watched amazed as it "crossed over" into that supposedly impenetrable general interest market. Peretti, whose books now have a posted average of 1.5 million copies sold per title, has recently signed a multimillion-dollar contract with WORD, Inc., for eleven new fiction titles, seven of them for children and all of them as crossovers.

Girzone and Peretti, though they were coming from different directions and operating out of different motivations, were the first to legitimize faith-initiated fiction as a major genre and to establish its presence in both general interest and religious bookstores, for just as Peretti proved to be a crossover onto the shelves of secular stores, so too did Girzone prove to be a huge success in cathedral, theological, and Evangelical Christian (i.e., CBA) bookstores. The audience they discovered and satisfied has continued to grow as the availability of their kind of fiction has become more generally known among the reading public; as more of it has come to be produced by skilled, professional writers; and, as I have already indicated, as there has been a proliferation of content subtypes employed.

Janette Oke, America's first lady of Evangelical Christian fiction, has established the historical or period inspirational novel as the linchpin of faith fiction, with sales of her books now in excess of 12 million copies and still rising. Brock and Bodie Thoene, who in 1993 signed an $11 million contract with Thomas Nelson for three new faith novels, are responsible for solidifying the place of both the western and the historical adventure story within the larger category of faith-motivated titles. The success by so many able writers with the romance novel subgenre within faith fiction has led Romance Writers of America (RWA), the organization of professional writers of secular romance fiction, to hold workshops on faith-oriented romance writing in conjunction with their national conventions. RWA is also considering ways of incorporating the subarea officially into its organizational structure.

All fiction, regardless of its type or origin, rests first upon the basic human principle that everybody loves a story and everybody wants to be entertained. There is no question about that. But when a section of storytelling develops its own aesthetic and can successfully superimpose upon basic human phenomenology an added agenda, and when, moreover, it succeeds at that unlikely endeavor so dramatically, logic cries out for some broader explanation than just human love for a story. The explanation seems to be that as a believing, seeking people, we believe in story as well as enjoy it.

We believe, that is, in the spirit of story, if not necessarily in its details. There is in story a potency of effect that frightens us while at the same time attracting us to its awful effectiveness. Joseph Campbell and Bill Moyers even gave a kind of intellectually acceptable face to our almost superstitious American sense that the Logos is resident in every well-told tale by showing us myth as a tool as well as a universal language. And certainly faith Fiction is unabashedly a tool. Faith fiction, be it westerns, mysteries, romances, adventures, or whatever else, always has some self-admitted purpose. For instance, much Evangelical Christian faith fiction is trying to change lives as they are being lived by changing the imaginative spaces of readers' entertainment time from guns, violence, bodice ripping, cursing, and wife beating to less graphic and contaminating treatments of these modern realities. Other forms of faith-initiated fiction can be more concerned with proselytizing than with behavior modification. Fr. Andrew Greeley spoke eloquently about this in a *New York Times Magazine* article[27] that in its full was called "Why Do Catholics Stay in the Church? Because of the Stories." One thinks likewise of authors like Susan Howatch, whose works gently persuade toward a denominationally specific tradition. Even Father Girzone, who began this whole thing as a successful commercial phenomenon, sees his Joshua as a means for "teaching Jesus." Not theology, not doctrine, not religion, he is equally quick to say, but Jesus the God/man.[28]

But quite apart from author and publisher motivations there is another problem. All the motivated writers and editors in the world can't sell a grouping of books — and especially not sell it so fulsomely — if there is not that other piece of the formula, the willing and eager audience. Who are we who read and read and stand in line to buy so we can read some more? And what holds us there? The answers to both those questions are becoming clearer every day.

Story from an Americans-over-thirty perspective is the soul in its nearest form. Whatever the effluence that grips us when we are within story, it is the same effluence that surrounds and perfumes the porches of the sacred. We know that affinity at a level that is fixed almost beyond the range of belief; know it as primal and indigenous cultures know it; know it as only a country that sings its poetry in syncopated lyrics can know it. We believe, and what we believe, above all else, is the Something that story suggests.

– 4 –

What We Are Seeking

TO BE A NATION OF BELIEVERS is as ennobling as the thing or things believed in — or as ignoble — for belief alone only focuses the attention and gives it parameters as well as a certain integrity to its actions. Seeking, on the other hand, still deals in possibilities; its impetus is some incompleteness or discontent that may or may not be subject to resolution. The energy of anxiety spices any quest and lends to it the teasing sweetness of failure's possibility or of resolution's benediction. Beliefs, in other words, only cordon off the areas initially open to search; desire for something envisioned that is not yet present fuels the hunt. And to the extent that desire can describe what it is that is yearned for within the bounded fields, so to that extent the chances of success are increased.

Since we who are adult in America today[1] pretty much know that we are inextricably caught up in a restive seeking, and since we have a reasonably accurate sense of what most of us believe in as the boundaries of the search as well as of why we think so, the question becomes one of whether or not we can describe what we're searching for. The answer to that one is absolutely. We do it all the time, all day every day in what we buy, what we chat about and seriously talk about, what we choose to watch and the magazines we choose to read. In a thousand informal decisions we tell each other and ourselves what we are seeking; we just think of that

LORETTE WILMOT LIBRARY
NAZARETH COLLEGE

process in considerably humbler terms. We think of all those daily expressions as being "what we want" and/or "what we need." Yet that much humbler, far more conversational ground of daily being, unpretentious and unimposing as it may be, is who and where we as generations within a culture really are. It is, therefore, or so it seems to me, where the real definition of what we are seeking is going to be found.

On the assumption that my day today as I write this or even my week to date has not been markedly distinguishable in its basics from that of most other adult Americans, and having put my attention deliberately to watching and listening as I passed through them — rather like Santa Claus, I thought to myself at one point, making a list and checking it twice, trying to find out — based, in other words, on a kind of back-of-the-envelop set of notations, I think that I can draw up a list of six or eight things that the vast majority of us are looking for or think we need, along with two or three added notions that we would, most of us, like to throw into the pot for extra good measure.

We want health. We are fixated there and have been for fifty years, ever since World War II and its resultant technology somehow conveyed to us that we both could be, and had a moral right to be, well. Which leads me to add that I think, if I am listening accurately, that what we really want is wellness. There is a considerable difference in the two that gets itself muddied by all our media-hyped and politically driven conversation about the mechanics of "health care," but what we want is wellness, of which health of body, mind, and society is certainly a part.

We want financial security. How that translates varies by race, locale, social class, sex, and so on. We all know the list of politically correct variables. One woman's fortune is another's poverty. But the central idea does indeed seem to be central: We want the wolf away from the door permanently and forever. That rewording, if it is accurate and I think it is, really means that we want the security and the permanently and the forever, but the money part is only a means to those ends. The money is almost a kind of shorthand for some of us and a limitation of vision for others of us, but very, very few of us seem to actually want money as an object to be admired on some shelf somewhere.

We want dominance. From the child pinching his unattended baby sister to the corporate CEO's jockeying for the presidency of a new conglomerate's board, we all want power over our circumstances and over each other. Unlike money that very quickly can be exposed as a tool in the wish lists of most of us, power is something we do want to set on the shelf and reverence, especially if we can manage to get up there and sit down beside it.

We want — one can almost say we *all* want — to be safe. Yet again, when one listens to what we are really saying in ordinary conversations to each other, one discovers that what we mean is that we want to be safe from one another. Natural disasters like flood, fire, and tornado are certainly part of our conversation, but for most of us they are the bases for dispassionate discussion and sometimes of reasoned precaution; they are not the stuff of daily, grinding concern. To fall victim to floods, fires and tornadoes, bad as that may be, is not as intimately ominous as to fall victim to holocaust or genocide or random violence or crime or immorality or unethical conduct or inner-familial disharmony or an oppressive circumstance or environment or even libelous and vicious gossip. These are the torments from which, colloquially, we would be safe.

We all — and this is the only item on my list with which I am confident of the correctness of *all* — we all want distraction from what eastern cultures call "monkey mind." We want sensations that divert us or activities that absorb us or purposes and events that focus us. Whatever the mechanism, in other words, we want to be relieved of self-awareness and self-commentary. The chatterer within, the monkey mind, the devil inside — whatever the name given — we want to escape him/it/them.

Many of us — and I suspect that this is true of most of us, but I cannot be sure—many of us need a sense of context or perhaps of a place within some context. It is almost the old "So, what about me?" or the "Where do I fit in?" question that, unanswered, leaves us feeling awkward, disenfranchised, and destructive of whatever is and/or is without us as constituent parts.

Likewise, many of us need or want a purpose. Logically, all of us have one, even if it is so fundamental a thing as maintaining ourselves for as long as possible. (Survival is hardly romantic as a life-focusing principle, though of course, and sadly for us, it was more than sufficient for our ancestors, as well as more than comforting.) The thing that has restricted wanting a sense of purpose to the status of many, as opposed to most, of us, in my listing, is that while purpose may indeed be a universal need, it is not always articulated by all of us. It is not even self-perceived by all of us. Yet I think we must, for the purposes of this part of our discussion anyway, be honest enough to include that which is routinely present among us, that which is so ubiquitously routine as to be the subtext, for example, of afternoon television or the slick weekly pages of *People.*

Additionally, I suspect that far more of us than would care to admit it want a style. Close to a perception of context and of where we fit into it, close to purpose, and certainly close to well-being, style — regrettably, I don't have a better word for it — is nearest perhaps to "signature" in its contemporary connotation, or at least to signatory behavior. We want to be Pygmalions sculpting ourselves. How we do that is dependent on how free we are to self-determine, just as how much we want to do it seems to be a function of station; but there are enough of us involved with achieving a style that it has to be put in the mix of the adult majority's wants and needs.

It seems to me, listening, that there are two other things that many of us would *like* to have added to our cup of blessings, despite the fact that we don't treat them in normal conversation and in routine decisions as being quite so central to us as the first eight are. The sad, odd, almost perverse thing about that degree of difference is that when we are thinking deliberately and speaking formally, we talk about both these values as very important. All of which is to say that beyond the biological imperatives of mating, life-partnering, and childbearing, we would like to love and we would like to be loved — probably in that order, if my sense of things is correct.

And that's pretty much the list of the things we seem to want or see ourselves as needing. Most other possibilities will subsume in one way or another under one of these ten. The remarkable thing about the ten, however, is not their ability to encompass, but rather how many of them are a result of progressive privilege. Health, sufficiency, dominance, and safety are primordial aims; the pursuit of distraction, context and style is a much more civilized concern, the expressed desire for answers to the "Who am I?" and the "How do I fit in?" questions having always been a gentleman's (or gentlewoman's) preoccupation; and the ability to stand outside experience in order to consider the need to love and be loved is downright leisured.

If nothing else, in other words, our list of adult American wants confirms what we already know: We, including even the poorest among us, compose, within our respective stations and comparatively speaking, the most privileged society in the world or in history. Our wants and needs, while they by bent of their origins can never escape being human, come nonetheless in the ordering and with the emphases of our circumstance.

But if this or any similar list of wants is going to facilitate our understanding of the sacred, the spiritual, and the religious among us today, it must first combine with the constructs of our beliefs and be translated out of the realm of either statistics or colloquial observations and into that of myth or story. That, as we have seen, is the American way.

*   *   *   *   *

A few saints, sadhus, and ecstatics to the contrary, not many human beings ever set out originally to discover the sacred. Instead, we discover, as we have seen, problems in our lives and holes in our understanding that set us to looking for solutions and illumination. What we find is a myriad of possibilities to be sorted through and selected from, so that we leave behind us a string of rejected goods like the bread-crumb trails of adventuresome children. It is at that point usually when, looking back over our shoulders, we realize that we are not where we were originally and so begin to interpret our movement in the images and figures of a physical journey, even creating for our movement the dignity of some possible destination.

Were we indeed children in a deep and vine-entangled forest, the majority of us — or so western heritage indicates — would yearn for the bluebird of happiness as, hungry and afraid and exhausted, we struggled down shadowed half trails toward a place of family. Ah, that family. It may not be complete in our modern sense of father, mother, and children, but it is inviolate, and our fairy tales give it a hundred different configurations. That family or part of a family is the heart of the western forest's foreboding depths.

Be their physical appointments a peasant cottage or a turreted castle, always there are warmth, food, and security with that family. Always there is a beautiful woman — beautiful as a princess is in youth and body, or beautiful as a godmother is in magic and power, or beautiful as a plump grandmother is in her wise affection and constancy. Always there is the clearing where the light is, and always the animals are fellow citizens within its activities. Sometimes there is a prince, a father, a woodsman, or a king. Sometimes there is an adventure or a purposed activity assigned. But always there is a forever after.

We hear such stories in the late afternoons and early evenings of our childhood, or we read them for ourselves in the small, short chairs of the public library, or we make them up for each other in the darkness of our bedrolls, or we sit on the living room floor on Saturday mornings with sleep-warm blankets pulled around us and watch them flash in front of us in gripping lines and colors. But always, in whatever guise we first meet and learn to keep them, always those stories of the forest journey and of the clearing at its center are like songs already sung within us. We recognize their plot as our own remembered future and become as engrossed in them as children do with any play that imagines them into life.

Like most mythic truth refined by centuries and passed along in our nursery years, the tale of the journey and its center are life in metaphor. The anima of the tale — the mercurial soul that informs it and runs through the fingers of comprehension like the teasing sand through the strictures of an hourglass — that essence is the indefinable constant.

Metaphor, on the other hand, is never constant, never a name, only a convenience of suggestion that employs a variousness of vehicle as well as of interpretation. When the question is couched in metaphor's terms, we can comfortably say that what we who are over thirty in America are seeking for is indeed the center that is housed in the metaphor. It is just that we understand the center better when it is housed, specifically, in our metaphors.

To speak of "our metaphors" is, of course, to imply some pleasant, cultural unanimity that probably has never existed on this continent and that most assuredly doesn't now. Thus the same story line, for those adult Americans whose Pueblo ancestors preceded the forest-dwelling Europeans to this landmass, varies its figures and details to coincide with the Pueblo terrain and experience.

In that first indigenous presentation of the story, there must be some error or sin on the part of the People that has forced the spirit to withdraw from them. Unable to travel to the Fourth World (that is, to the center), the People send Flying Hummingbird, rather than the bluebird of happiness, as emissary. Flying

Hummingbird journeys to the heart of the earth to petition the spirit that light and blessing may return to the People. The spirit is, in the Pueblo telling of the story, always female in personification and may be called either the Grandmother or the Mother of the People.

Either way, Flying Hummingbird's petition cannot and will not be granted until the People do reverence to the Grandmother spirit in all their actions, intentions, and thoughts. Only when they are purified by amendation, humility, and obedience will the People be ready once more to receive the spirit back among them. Flying Hummingbird delivers the Grandmother's message, the People obey, and all is in balance once more until such time as the People err and the journey must be repeated.

The Pueblos' is a wonderful variation of the journey, as powerful as the forest variation and having for many of us a much greater harmony of its details, especially the geographic ones, with those of our own experiences. In much the same way the oldest nonindigenous rendering of the journey story informing contemporary American perceptions is the Jewish Exodus. The Haggadah may tell of Zion instead of a clearing and of a mountain instead of a meadow or valley. It may have a pillar of fire and a cloud of smoke in the sky instead of birds. It may have Balaam's ass as befriending counselor instead of spotted deer. But it's the same story.

At a practical level, however, we can't, in so short a space as this, deal with all the variations upon a theme if we are ever to get on with the theme itself. Since the forest clearing variation is central to most of us and/or — very decisive factor — central to most children's television and comic books, it seems to be the most sensible choice for considering how our understanding of the seeking journey has been adapted by our times.

One of the more significant of those specific adjustments in our metaphorical equipment here and now as opposed to elsewhere and before is that we see ourselves as perhaps containing the forest. We are forced by our own enlightenment to ask, as those who originally described their journey in terms of the forest never were, whether or not we are ourselves making those deep woods or projecting them or domesticating them or doing some combination of all three. The result — and it is the result that distinguishes our search from past ones in western culture — the result is that what we look for first is a way to bring ourselves through a part of ourselves and into the clearing. We need, moreover, a method or mapping for that process that will work not just once but every day and upon demand. We assume, in other words, that to live is to travel back and forth through the forest that may be ourselves; and we think that we can endure repetitious travel if only we can return from time to time and more or less at will to the nurturing sanctuary of the cottage, the family, and the ministering lady of our inherited fairy tales.

The second metaphorical difference for us now — semisophisticates that we are and space adventurers by culture and television if not by actuality — is that we are the possessors and processors of many worlds, the worlds in our head, the worlds of our biological lives, the worlds in our possibilities and our probabilities. What we know we have to have before we can travel to the clearing is a connection between all these realms, a way almost of stacking all those realities upon one another like so many transparencies in overlay in order that they may be seen in register — or sometimes more urgently sought — in order that we can be sure they are capable of register and that some greater frame forever holds them there.

A third and remarkable difference between us and those early seekers who first spun the metaphors of the journey, the forest, and the familied center is a difference between us and the intervening great-great-grandparents through whom we have received the stories. It is a difference once more of neoprimalism. The first storytellers were themselves in toto. The intervening relayers of the tales were, however, enlightened and thereby segmented; and their enlightened rhetoric of the body as machine has turned at last to dust and like dust has blown away. We know beyond all doubt that the flesh is not just vehicle for the soul. If nothing else, a half century of technologized medicine has taught us that in protracted, bitter lessons. The flesh, we whisper sotto voce to ourselves and a few trusted others, may *be* the soul and, like it, an expression of the spirit. The ancients, now no more than memories on the forest verge, smile and nod. It is the shades of the great-grandparents who scowl.

There is a fourth adaptation of our perceptions of the mythic story that is likewise a consequence of the Enlightenment, and that is that we don't see either evil or magic in the same way that those first tellers of the tale apparently did. The former we see as a result of human action more than as an embodied agent with personality and purposes of its own. The latter we see as being explicable in most instances and, in the remainder, as requiring a kind of testing and retesting for efficacy and refinement before it can be accepted at its claimed value.

I suspect also — though one cannot be sure — that we are the first descendant generations to approach the forest stories as containing something beyond themselves. Stories that admittedly may have arrived a century or two ago at a stage of being culturally canonical are now — and I suggest for the first time — quite literally so. I suggest also that the journey to the clearing in the center is as scriptural as the Exodus in terms of our expectations of them both.

What that shift speaks to is a popular recognition of, and comfort with, the difference that exists between the sacred and the divine. To be able to make that distinction at the lay level is a spiritual nicety we should all be proud of and rejoice over. The existence of that kind of newfound subjective sophistication as part of our daily lives is also, by the way, one of the reasons I suspect our own age of being another time of renaissance and part of the basis for my predicting that our passage through it will be a good and blessed one. Meanwhile, if the forest story is the veil of metaphor, then perhaps we can draw it aside to discover the configurations of the sacred just as surely as Jews and Christians have been able to pull aside the Exodus and expose the hand of God.

– 5 –

What We Believe the Sacred Is

I HAD A PROFESSIONAL ASSOCIATE a number of years ago who was somewhere between an acquaintance and a friend. We interacted, in other words, in that space where there is no real intimacy but all the comforts of familiarity. Being neither a Christian nor an agnostic in a culture whose citizens usually define themselves by one or the other, he chose instead to refer to himself as a believer. His explanation of that cryptic self-description was that he believed that when one dies, the clouds pull apart and in the center where they had been "is a placard saying '2 + 2 = 4,' but we just don't know what that means yet."

"2 + 2 = 4, but we just don't know what that means yet" struck me originally, and still strikes me now, as one of the very few profound things anybody has ever said to me. I have rolled it about in my thoughts for years, the way one rolls a lucky marble or a highly polished worry stone, and it has remained as obvious and obscure as they both are.

"2 + 2 = 4, but we just don't know what that means yet" is also the best one-sentence description of the sacred I have ever heard or could ever hope to invent. The problem with it, of course, is that it is too polished, too profound. One would need years to arrive honestly at the flavor of its pure concentrate. For most of us, a few more words and a lot more dilution are good and necessary things in dealing with the mysterium.

* * * * *

Adolescence, as we remember it and observe it in the children maturing around us, is a time of a thousand agonies — every day. Were we forced to reduce all of its turmoils into a single definition, we would say that adolescence is a time of dislocation: Dislocation of sociability from one arena of possibilities and one homogeneous, morally predictable community to an open range of erratic, roaming possibilities and a constantly shifting, constantly self-referencing series of communities.

Dislocation of the body from an asexual, essentially undifferentiated, and unobtrusive one to a raucously present, maintenance-requiring one that, for better or for worse, every one of us is for life, without any hope of parole.

Dislocation of consciousness (as if self-awareness like sexuality were also hormone-spurred) from an immediate and companionable one to a detracting, discursive, combative one; a dislocation, in other words — and the most painful one at that — in which the imaginary friend of kindergarten is evicted by the restive chatterer, and monkey mind takes over.

We emerge — most of us[1] — from those transitional, dislocating years of adolescence aware of a kind of chronic ache that, like a rheumatism of the soul, will neither leave us nor entirely disable us. As an ache it hovers between a low-grade discomfort and a full-fledged yearning. We wander back and forth between the two extremes, but we interpret the ache as arising from a single principle: Once there was a unity that now is gone. And its corollary: That same unity is the sacred.

Not God — although divinity almost immediately gets closely tied into the discussion for most of us — not God, but that presumed, and presumably remembered, oneness that in its living, brilliant particularities is a companionable whole. That is the sacred. And whether we speak of individual experience in phrases like "the loss of innocence" or of speciel experience in stories like the Garden of Eden one, we mean only to symbolize our separateness from it while at the same time asserting our historic right to mourn for it as something once enjoyed and now lost.

In and from that backward-longing, loss-professing stance, we define our lives through the metaphors of search and quest and journey, and ourselves as travelers upon an often tenuous trail in or up toward the consummation — toward, that is, our reconnection.

The distinction between trails in and trails up is an important one, despite the fact that the sacred presumably is the same whether we conceptualize it horizontally or vertically. Likewise, the end result of our effort in the seeking presumably is the same regardless of the axis we choose for our travel. The truth is that in actual practice most of us see the sacred as both "in" and "up" anyway (although not simultaneously), and we move freely back and forth between the two conceptualizations at will and with no apparent sense of contradiction.

We speak a great deal in America today, for example, about centering. As a presently in vogue, subjective buzzword, *centering* is good for talking about just about everything from meditating on the mind of the Buddha to slipping back for a little rest into the forest clearing. That is, it gives a name to the intentional gathering of the attention *in*to one focus that in its quietness, like a glass lens held to the sun, will burn a hole in the obstructing membrane between now and no time — a recognition, geographic in every way possible, that the sacred is somehow within us.

We routinely seek aesthetic or ecstatic experiences too as a means of subjective "transport," essentially predetermining our direction by our choices. The simple, muffled repetitions of a tom-tom, for instance, are far more horizontal and "centering" than the resounding, hierarchical bombast of the Hallelujah Chorus (which, by the way, we regard as well done in direct proportion to its ability to "uplift" us — an equally geographic and positional metaphor).

Even more popular among us — or simply more talked about when we yearn for the sacred — is the retreat. Be it a trek to some less inhabited physical spot like the mountains and woods that lift the heart up "unto the hills from whence cometh our help," or to an ancestral place where communal faith has hallowed a doorway by its constant trafficking *in,* our search uses such means to know the surcease of our sorrow.

To merge into a kind process once more, into an allness without prejudice or pain, into the dance of Life as aware celebrants of it/us/each other, that is the aim; for the sacred, when we glimpse it and regardless of the direction by which we approach it, is that constant that holds, that centering post around which all else swirls in orchestrated fractals and from which all else depends. It is neither of personality nor without it but rather is that perfection of the imagination, a living principle always and everywhere applicable while always and forever like and unlike itself. It is, as my late associate so fully realized, "2 + 2 = 4" in all of its unknowable and enrapturing grandeur; its simplicity begs even the question of our own amazement and we cannot attain to it.

* * * * *

The sacred that is, and that can reveal itself within creation as 2 + 2 = 4, can be seen as sufficient. Such sufficiency is, as the Hebrew psalmist said, "too wonderful for us." And there are on this earth billions and within this country millions of human beings who hold the sufficiency — the Tao, the process, the Brahman, the by whatever name — as itself.

There are millions more — and in this country the greater percentage of our millions — for whom the sacred is not just the terrain of mystery but also the evidence of an intimate mysterium; people who would say, as I did to my acquaintance, "Ah, but 2 *times* 2 also equals 4," and who, not quite understanding what that means but knowing deeply that it does have meaning, slip down quietly like fish diving into the harbor's darkened depths to follow the flashing, silvery tails of those who have embraced the sea before them.

And then there are those among us who, believing in the journey and in both the forest clearing and the mountaintop and in the sacred positioned there, see them all as no more than anterooms. Call it by whatever name and symbolize it by whatever architecture, the sacred is only the semiprivate space appointed by the lord of the manor for doing business with his retainers and beyond which none of them is ever destined to go save by grace and disciplined petition.

But as diverse and sometimes mutually exclusive as these various ways of perceiving the sacred may be, they all agree on one thing: reverence. The immutable sacred will be, and it will be reverenced. Those who would contemplate its elegance and those who would merely do business with it and all those stretched out in between — all must come first to reverence. Moreover, those foolish beings who fail in reverence eventually are not, as foam thrown against the sea wall is not, or light against the dark side of the moon is not. From the conditions given Flying Hummingbird by the Grandmother to the moral codes of Sinai to the mindfulness of the Buddhist monk to the opening salvo "hallowed be thy Name," there is always, when we approach the sacred, the same singing theme: reverence. Be still and know.

*   *   *   *   *

Reverence can give expression to itself in many ways, some of them religious but not all of them so and certainly not all of them requisitely so; for reverence is an attitude, a posture of the whole person, that may begin and end with itself or may extend to incorporate a whole panoply of glad oblations.

My realization of that rich variety of possibilities has grown over the years of my own maturing, of course, but my first significant, penetrating introduction to it occurred on an afternoon, well over twenty years ago now, when I was living and working in Mexico for a summer. That one dramatic experience so purged my mind of all its habitual sureties that it became a parable for me; and I have never since been able to approach reverence, either as a concept for discussion or as a practice for my own private employment, except in terms of a few, brief hours in the mountainous country of the Sierra Madre.

The telling of that story, however, is not, as was the case with the axiom of my now deceased associate, a matter of mere anecdote. Quite the contrary. As becomes reverence, the story of my first true introduction to its many faces requires the leisure of some quieter space. It requires the interruption of an interlude.

— Interlude —

A Parable

I T SEEMS TO ME that I had been in the Sierra Madre of Mexico, that high country of ineffable beauty, for no more than a week or so. I am not sure. Whatever the length of time, however, it had not been sufficient for me to become accustomed to the practice of the siesta, although my intellect had already begun to grasp its wisdom. Uncharacteristically, my landlady for the summer, a genteelly impoverished widow of Castilian descent, had deferred early to the heat that day and was dozing beneath the foliage of her patio well before one o'clock. As much out of courtesy to her as out of any genuine energy or restiveness, I left her there and, opening the massive wooden doors that secured us from the cobbled streets, slipped outside into the sterilizing light of one of Mexico's more rigorous summers.

Beyond me, the town of Saltillo was itself in siesta, all its faces turned inward to their own dreams, all its walls blank of human expression. I was alone. Indeed, I was bereft — bereft certainly of my landlady, whose quirky humor and low tolerance for gringas I had already come to depend upon for entertainment.

But if my landlady's disposition had turned out to be of a rather acerbic turn — and undeniably Sophia de los Fuentes y González's had — she herself had proved more flexible than most who are so turned. She had, in fact, already done me the honor of suspending, at least for one summer, her inviolate prejudices against all things Yankee. She had done this for one reason and one reason only: I

70

loved going to *la catedral* as much as she did, though not for the same reasons.

In the clear dawns of Saltillo's high-mountain days, Sophia's wooden doors were always the first to open; she and I, always the first to step down together into the dusty street on our way to early mass. In the orange of late afternoon, Sophia's silhouette was the first to move across the roof walks, moving toward *la catedral*, with me picking my way cautiously behind her. In midevening, when the bells of compline or vespers began pealing across the housetops, it was Sophia, with me in tow, who made her way like a shade bending, holding close to the patio walls and avoiding the alley parties, going for one last time toward *la catedral* . . . she toward her prayers and I toward the more emotional sanctuary of sacred memories and cloistered shadows. But in this, too, Sophia was willing to accept my digressions. If I were not Roman Catholic, I was at least Anglican, and that seemed, in Sophia's thinking, to be some kind of exonerating justification for all my offenses.

To be Anglo under any set of conditions was suspect to Sophia. She was very sure, for instance, that to be Anglo and Roman Catholic at the same time was an apostasy, a bastardization of the one true faith, a contradiction in applied loyalties, an intolerable mix of contrarieties. But Anglicanism, ah, now that was a different matter. Anglicanism, in Sophia's scheme of things, was the religious deprivation one should have to endure in recompense for having been born Anglo. But by practicing it, I was at least being consistent. Consistency is a moral virtue. Therefore, it seems, I was living with integrity; and by virtue of my integrity, I was acceptable. (I was also Sophia's first Anglican, a fact for which I was more than passingly grateful during all the days and nights I lodged under her roof, boarded at her table, and trooped behind her back and forth over the kilometer and a half that separated her house from the courtyard of *la catedral*.)

All of which is by way of explaining what I did, and why, on that white, white afternoon when I was bereft and wandering in a town I did not yet truly know and in a light I wanted only to escape. It was, in other words, a new habit combined with a life-long love of shadows that took me to *la catedral* that day. The relief of its mullioned narthex was immediate and welcoming, but it was as nothing compared to the cooling gloom of the cathedral's cavernous interior.

Without Sophia as guide, I had to wait a moment or two at the rear of the nave for my eyes to grow used to the half gloom of candles and tapers and clerestoried light. Then, following the practice that she and I had already followed so many times to-gether, I turned left and walked down the aisle toward the lectern on the gospel side of the chancel. At first I had thought I was alone in the place. Certainly in the hour of siesta I was expecting no noise other than my own thoughts and no movements other than those of my own feet. As I got nearer to the transept and as my eyes accommodated, however, I realized I was wrong.

In the cathedral of Saltillo, as in so many Roman churches, a statue of the Virgin stood, elevated in benediction, on the gospel, or left, side of the center aisle. Because this was a cathedral and no ordinary church, however, Saltillo's statue was hardly a modest one. Rather it was an elaborately rendered one of fairly massive proportions. Had Our Lady been at eye level, I might have been better able to accurately gauge her size, but even positioned as she was, there could be little question that she stood at least six and a half feet tall, if not more, and that her outstretched hands extended themselves in perfect proportion to her height.

Unlike the statuary that I had been accustomed to in North American churches, Saltillo's Virgin was robed, not in some painted-on garb, you understand, but in a luxuriant costuming of cloth of gold, velvet, and rich damasks, with linings to every-thing of ivory-hued satins. The orphreys of her outer robe alone were a king's ransom in brocade, and the silk tracings embroi-dered on her hemline were of an intricacy beyond my powers of discovery. It was, therefore, something of an affront for me to realize, as I began to see her more clearly, that Our Lady was, like me, bereft — bereft of all her finery and of her linen tunic as well. Then I heard them.

There were four of the women, and their sound at first was like the noise of aging mice — light, scurrying, unobtrusive, but no longer afflicted by a predatory fear. They worked by the light of the chancel candles and by such light as might indeed drift to them from the clerestories above and beyond them, but they worked without agitation. Their noise was a hum rather than an articulation; and though they were a group, they seemed almost as unaware of one another as they were of me, each worker being removed into her own cloister of needles and tauting thread.

Our Lady's robe lay carefully opened on the transept floor, a carpet of blue tissues beneath it as protection against the foot dust of four centuries. When I first perceived them through the gloom, two of the women were still about the business of tidying the robe. One was snipping away infinitesimal (or perhaps imaginary — I couldn't tell) bits of raveled lining and frayed brocade. The other had what appeared to be a solvent of some sort in one hand and a clean rag in the other. She was dusting — I know no other word for it — the robe in great, broad, kissing strokes, removing from it any hint of soil or stasis.

A third woman, smaller than the others, more bent upon herself and more shrouded than they in the head scarf of the devout peasant, was stooped to her work on Our Lady's tunic. The tunic itself lay across the lap and up over the right shoulder of a fourth and slightly younger woman, whose torso was being used as a worktable as well as a protection against both sacrilege and soil. While the younger held the tunic up and its hemline taut, the elder scrutinized its embroidery, stitch by stitch, stopping now and then to snip an errant thread and once to replace what appeared, from my distance, to be a break in the pattern.

How long the women had been at their work before I came upon them I could not say; but they appeared to have almost completed it. I eased off the kneeler from which I had been studying them and sank my weight back onto the pew behind me, watching, more in lassitude than with any real interest, this strange and, to me, near-pagan process of dressing an icon.

The women were occupied with their refurbishing and repairs for no more than another five to ten minutes before I began to sense a change in them, a kind of gathering in of excitement. Certainly they became more animated and more a part of one another.

The Virgin's tunic, so soon as its repairs had been completed to the women's satisfaction, was vigorously, but reverently, shaken to remove any wrinkles and then laid with a painful exactitude precisely atop her velvet robe, which had been left in its place on the transept floor. When I had come into the nave, there had been a ladder propped against the chancel wall, and I had surmised, correctly, that the women had used it to remove the garments they were working on. Now, as if in confirmation, two of them moved the ladder back into position nearer the statue, propping it against the arch just behind Our Lady but in easy reach of her body.

While the ladder was being set into place, a third woman — the younger one who had so impassively held the hem of the tunic taut and extended while it was being cleaned — quietly knelt down in the transept floor and, as I looked on, pulled from its place beneath the railing a *bolsa,* one of those cloth sacks that peasants use, much as we use backpacks in our country, to hold everything. This one was obviously old, badly in need of replacement, and thin with its mistress's impoverishment.

«¿Ahora?» ("Now?")

She had said the word over her shoulder to her companions, and it was the first word I had heard any of them speak, the first distinguishable sound they had made to each other in the quarter hour since I had been watching them.

The older woman nodded her head in assent. «Ahora.»

I heard the tissue's lively rustle before I actually saw it. The two women were so bent to the work of its extrication, so reverential in their concern over it, that they alone were visible at first. As they stood up, I could see the flat packet of blue tissue and even the hank of soft market twine that held it. Whatever the packet contained, it was limp, in and of itself, and of no great size.

Wordlessly, one of the women at the base of the ladder began to mount it while the second held it steady. As soon as she had climbed up to the height of the Virgin's head, the woman on the ladder turned back toward the other three still below her. They now took the packet and, with the younger woman supporting it carefully on her upturned palms, they began to unwrap first its twine and then its interleaving layers of blue tissue.

What emerged was intended as a garment obviously, something closest to what I would call a chemise of sorts, though it lacked thin straps and had instead much broader shoulder supports. It was not the object itself, however, or its use that riveted me; it was the women. One by one they kissed the skirt of the chemise, passing it from one to another as it moved toward the fourth and last woman waiting on the ladder. She, having likewise kissed the garment's hem, gently lifted the whole up and settled it down over the body of the statue.

The chemise was of string, of some kind of glossy and apparently tightly spun string, that almost glistened with the luster of its own twist. Had I been asked to identify the process of its manufacture, I would have said it was tatting, though I am relatively sure that there was a far more intricate knotting process involved — more intricate, that is, than that which the word usually connotes. Without seams anywhere, the chemise was a perfect harmony of lacework by whatever method, its open spaces held in exquisite and secure balance between its knotted tracings. The whole was breathtaking, not just because of the months it must have taken the four women to construct and fashion it — certainly that was arresting once I had begun to understand the investment it must have constituted for the four of them — no, the chemise was breathtaking as an object.

Never before had I ever seen anything so beautiful, so perfected to its purposes, so angel-like in its effect. Mary was no longer an icon or a statue; she was all things good; she was the Good. Energy flowed from her in a rush of urgent peace like the pent-up joy of birth itself, and I could say nothing. I wanted to. I wanted to stand up at least, to cry out to the women, "Look! Look! I'm here too, and it's good — so good! — this thing that you have done." Instead I could do nothing, paralyzed beyond even prayer by exaltation. And in that moment of my own transport I saw on their faces the same astonishment before what they had created, the same loss of everything except transport itself. Then the moment faded — or more correctly, then its emotions became identifiable. The women softened from glory into joy, their bodies eased from the erectness of passion down into the shapes and stances of contentment.

As if in response to some shared but unspoken ordering, the three women still standing at the base of the ladder moved together to lift Our Lady's tunic from its place on the transept floor. Kissing it as they had earlier kissed the chemise, they passed the tunic up to the waiting hands of their companion. Then came the robe itself. After that there was only the putting away of the ladder, the folding up of all the tools and pieces of used tissue, the closing of the *bolsa*. The work was done; and as soon as it was done, their gift — their unspeakable gift of devotion — was completely hidden.

* * * * *

«¿Qué pasa, querida?» ("What's wrong, my dear?") It was Sophia's voice coming to me from a very long way away. We were alone in her kitchen, eating our supper by lamplight at her kitchen table; and I realized that I had no idea what I was eating or had been eating, nor any idea of what we had been talking about.

«¿Qué pasa?» she asked me again, and I told her.

I told her about the women, about the chemise, about the intensity of my reaction to it. "It was," I said, "it was as if their faces glowed with her, as if their very bodies cried out, 'See how much we have loved her! How much of ourselves we have caught and fastened here! With how much of glory our own hands have dressed her!' "

Sophia waited and I struggled to find some way of touching again the extravagant emotions of my afternoon. "Do you remember," I asked her at last, "those words of the Christ during his Triumphant Entry? How he looked out over the shouting multitude and said to his disciples, 'I tell you that, if these should hold their peace, the stones would immediately cry out'?"

She nodded and, for once, held her own peace, as if she were inviting me to go on.

"I never understood those words until this afternoon," I said, and knew the instant the words were out of my mouth that I had just spoken the truth. I had never accepted the rejoicing of stones, not until those few suspended minutes among Saltillo's when every part of *la catedral*'s nave had raised itself in ascendancy around me; not until four peasant women, settling a tunic like a curtain over a thing of beauty, had silenced the mighty chorus of a pure antiphony.

«¿Y?» Sophia asked. ("And?")

"And I guess I feel" — I hesitated, trying to locate what it was I did feel. Drained? Let down? Disturbed? No, none of those. "I guess what I am feeling is a kind of grief that the moment is gone forever and that no one else will ever see the chemise again. Maybe I am a little bit angry for the women's sake — maybe I am a lot angry even, for me as well as them — that so much work and so much beauty can just be covered up before it is ever even seen, much less appreciated."

"But the women know," Sophia said. My face must have shown her how unsatisfactory a solution I found that to be, because she went on speaking in a tone and manner that were almost motherly and that were most certainly kindly. "Don't confuse your experience with the women's, *querida*. They have served Our Lady. You have not."

"I've no access to icons, Sophia, and no way of knowing what maintaining them involves."

"No, no, no!" — Sophia's whole body became her old, impatient self again — "Not the statue! Our Lady! *¡La estatua es una estatua solamente!* [The statue is only a statue.] Just as your chemise is only a chemise *y no más* [a chemise and nothing more]!" The black eyes glinted with the fervor of Sophia's annoyance, and then, just as abruptly, they softened. "But Our Lady? Ah, *querida,* Our Lady is, and that is the triumph that the women serve."

I remembered Mary in that moment when the chemise had first dropped over her — remembered how, in that absolutely opened instant, she had seemed to me to be, as Sophia said, neither a statue nor a theory, but good. I remembered precisely and with a returning breathlessness, in fact, that in those few seconds she had seemed to me to be the Good, and that by that term I had meant something that I could recognize but that I could in no way give name to.

"Yes," I admitted. "Yes, I know that in some way beyond just 'is' she is. Or at least I know that I understood something close to that this afternoon in the cathedral."

Sophia nodded her acceptance of my attempt to follow her, and we sat alone for a short while in silence. The kerosene lantern, which was that night, just as on every other night, lit on the kitchen cabinet behind us, sputtered a bit. Sophia looked up at it a minute and then said almost dreamily, "Tell me. The lamp there, do you think of it as the light?"

"Of course not."

"And if I blow it out, is it the lamp you feel concern for?"

"Of course not, again."

"Exactly," Sophia said, and there was just a hint of Castilian hauteur back in her voice for the first time in a quarter hour. "If I blow out the flame, you are full of concern for yourself, for what you have lost. You suddenly have a great hunger for the beautiful light, but the lamp is of no importance to you. Oh, touching it in the darkness or even seeing its outline through the window's gloom might help you. They might comfort you and reassure you that once upon a time there had been light here with us and that, as long as you have the lamp, the light could and might come again. But that is not how it is for the women in *la catedral.*

"The women in *la catedral* have tended Our Lady and made her chemise. It was theirs before it held her. Their adoration, if you will, made the lamp for her light — and, *querida,* when one has been the lamp, the maker and tender of the lamp, the very stuff even of which the lamp is, then one knows the light. One has held it against one's heart as the glass chimney contains the flame. One always sees the light differently after that."

There was silence again in Sophia's kitchen, each on us lost on that space where no words and all knowing meet. "There is one other thing," Sophia said, and her voice seemed to me far away this time because she herself was. "There is one other thing I can tell you. It is easier for the women than it will ever be for you. We are so poor here that they have nothing except themselves, so there is nothing except themselves to give away. For you, it will never be so simple." And she began to clear away the plates. Our supper was ended.

– 6 –

How We Approach
the Sacred

THE SACRED IS. Humanity has always known that, in whatever place and whatever time humanity has itself been. Humanity has also suspected — and philosophers have made their reputations by declaring — that the desideratum, or the thing desired, and the sacred were co-created and co-creative. That is to say, in a kind of maddening circularity of illogic, that we desire what we desire and then label our desideratum as "good" or "sacred" because we desire it; but we are driven to ultimate desiring and to our expressions of it by the immutable and inescapable principles of the sacred itself.[1] Thus, the symbol and the symbolized are both the same and ineluctably dissimilar.

What is new about this state of affairs, then, is not its presence in the archives of human understanding but its presence as a generalized, workaday perception in American culture. Until Joseph Campbell began to talk (and until Bill Moyers, who could make what Joseph Campbell saw comprehensible to a broad segment of us, began to film), the American sense of the sacred was largely a parochial one.

We Americans had little perspective from which to grasp the circularity of the sacred and the human, just as there had been almost no prior grasp for Rosie and Johnny of a universal unconsciousness, much less of what such a concept could mean.

80

It is equally fair and necessary, of course, to admit that neither Bill Moyers nor all the pervasive mediums of television, videos, and richly illustrated books and journals in the world could have turned what Jung and Campbell saw into a matter of cultural impact and popular concern all by themselves. That confluence of circumstances that we have already discussed and that has shaped our late-twentieth-century culture and our generations within it had to come first. It was the combination of prior circumstances, facile articulators, and roiling upheaval that made us ready recipients for messages from the gods; but as a result of that singular combination, it mattered almost not at all which gods they were. Any would do.

When Campbell, his students, his predecessors, and his successors began to show, in an enormously accessible and therefore very persuasive way, that myth speaks species-ial and canonical, but not sectarian, truths, they introduced an obvious and ancient perception. It was just simply a perception that had failed to get on the boat with the exiting European Pilgrim Fathers and that had not been missed by them (and most definitely had not been missed by their descendants, who were caught in a culture too concerned with physical and political survival to contemplate the sacred in any way much beyond that of practical manipulation).

What Campbell and company did in introducing to a popular audience the implications of, and the bases of credible proofs for, a co-creative relationship between the sacred and our human articulation of it was only one, however, of the two great shocks that were to strip American thinking of much of its subjective naiveté and certainly of its parochialism. The second was the discovery, again at a popular level, that the sacred does not have to be engaged theistically; or put positively, the sacred can be engaged nontheistically.

Not only did such an idea never get on the *Mayflower* in the first place, but it would undoubtedly have been drowned at sea had it been discovered stowed away there. But a shrinking world, all those Asian wars and war marriages, immigration and emigration, and so on rectified the insults of past time. At the very moment when frontier religion seemed most superfluous and Enlightenment theology most arid, there came among us from abroad and back among us from their disenfranchisements and reservations several million new, old, and original Americans who on a daily basis reverenced: Americans who believed quietly and comprehensively in the sacred; who governed their lives with fastidiousness; who deliberately and at all times exercised reverence and drew from it an exquisite morality *and who never felt compelled to say the word "God" in order to accomplish any of these things.*

And if America's over-thirties did not intend to live nontheistically as a consequence, we certainly did intend to investigate extensively the lives and ways of those who do. From Vine Deloria, Jr.'s *God Is Red* (which first published in 1972 and is now something of a classic in the field) to the present moment, there has been an ever-expanding flow of highly successful, highly visible books on Native American reverence. Even more inundating has been the flood of volumes, on the bestseller lists and off, of texts on Buddhism and Zen Buddhism. These nontheistic approaches have not only produced some of our generation's most-read, most-treasured books but even spawned a whole subsection of our publishing industry.[2]

If the sacred and the religious were not forever severed from one another by all of this free-form, do-it-yourself exploration of other ways (as of course they could not be for very long, much less forever), they were certainly well on their way to being differentiated from one another by means of it. And while the sacred was soon very much like unto a thing released from a long entombment, throwing bandages and strips of winding cloths everywhere, religion, especially institutional religion, was showing every sign of an incipient dormancy rather like that of a caterpillar spinning painfully down toward its chrysalis stage.

To those like Sophia de los Fuentes y González who were looking in at us from afar and from the perspectives of a deeper
civilization while all of this was beginning to bubble and boil,
we Americans must indeed have appeared pathetic and comical
as well as ugly. Yet the telling thing for me — and I can only hope
that it is an accurate perception rather than a merely chauvinistic
one — the telling thing about Sophia's instruction of me was not
her metaphor of the lamp, insightful as that may have been, but
her assessment of the relative difficulty for me as a white, middle-
class American, as opposed to that of the Saltillo peasant women,
in discovering a way to become chimney to the light.

Every Christian knows the Beatitudes and recognizes in them a
religious statement of the same principle — "Blessed are the poor,"
and so on. In a way, every sidewalk philosopher recognizes the
same principle also, as does almost every other religious and/or
wisdom system in the world. So Sophia's point was not new to
me, or to anybody else for that matter. What was new, however —
what neither she nor I knew in the late sixties — was that a self-
conscious, intentional, deliberated engagement of the sacred can
become as powerful and as sinewy as a naive engagement of it is;
and what I think neither of us could possibly have even guessed,
much less known, back then was just how powerful and sinewy
such an engagement was going to become in North American
practice during the last three decades of this millennium.

Even more revelatory is what neither Sophia nor I factored in
in our supper conversation but that I at least should have known.
(It was certainly right under my *norteamericana* nose and, most
ironic of all, I was at the time on the faculty of a college in
Memphis, Tennessee, the home of Elvis Presley and the world
headquarters for COGIC, the Church of God in Christ.)

What Sophia and I did not factor in was how immigrant African and Mediterranean Christianities would combine in America's migrant and blue-collar underclass to create an ecstatic
reverence very like that of the women in the cathedral of Saltillo,

in its effect if not in its overt expressions. And what she and I really did not even begin to grasp — what history itself had had no prototype for[3] — was how in a democratic and open society like the American one, Pentecostal "soul" could and would blend in with primarily middle-class, primarily North European, Protestant Christianity and Judaism to create an entirely new kind of seeker after the sacred.

That seeker without precedent is us; and our searches are, in aggregate and individually, eclectic with a breadth and range that beg even the word itself. There is hardly a sacral purist among us; and though I cannot prove it, I suspect that there's not a single, solitary "class" or "station" purist in Sophia's sense. That is, there is none in the sense of a seeker so restricted by position, birth, or circumstance as to be denied any hope of irrational or ecstatic reverence on a daily and welcomed basis.

What is incredible, almost shocking, and certainly unique here as we enter the third millennium is America's egalitarian soul. We seek by every means shamelessly, building our own individual methods with, and concepts of, the sacred rather as we build our salads at the local fern bar: a little heart of artichoke humbled by a few kidney beans, the garbanzos and fillets of anchovy kept honest with english peas, the jalapeños tempered in their enthusiasms by sliced, bland mushrooms, and the whole thing given cultural ballast by black olives and kohlrabi leaves. We have become a nation of uninhibited subjective gourmands.[4]

But whether the sacred is seen theistically or nontheistically and whether it is approached ecstatically or cerebrally makes no difference to that one immutable principle with which we began: Admission to the sacred presupposes reverence. And like that to which it serves as bodyguard and lover, reverence too can be effected theistically or nontheistically, ecstatically or cerebrally, or as is the case among us now, on a sliding scale that mixes and matches a little of all of them into its own means of exercise. The only thing that seems to matter is that each of us should find the form or forms of reverence from which we can construct our own trail of bread crumbs into the forest clearing with its comforting community, its beautiful lady, its serene mystery, and its terrible possibilities.

*   *   *   *   *

Reverence is the intercourse of life with life, the consummate art of union with the obliterating constant. Both an attitude and an action, reverence becomes in time a being, a state of whole and quiet knowing, and an enjoying of the bounds of creatureness.

Reverence is the peace of bowing to that which is so other-than-oneself as to encompass the self, so beyond form and handle that bowing is no diminishment, only fulfillment. It is acceptance of the immutable with an acceptance that releases, almost as if the restricting milkweed pod were broken at last and its million tiny selves were broadcast like angels in the rupture.

Reverence is an understanding of order and an embracing of it. It is the taking up with grace of one's inescapable place in the process of life. It is walking in balance.

Reverence is not only the walking, however, but also the template that allows one to accomplish the walking. Or put more humbly, it is a pair of spectacles through which one sees the fixed worthiness of the physical world and the appointed grandeur of the nonphysical one and is empowered thereby to participate in both of them appropriately.

Reverence is trust that informs the every gesture and decision of any life that feels it and that finds expression for itself in every controlled act; for reverence ultimately is control and a means given for self-control, just as love itself controls and self-controls. But reverence is not love; it is a cooler force, not an emotion, and lacks love's passion.

Reverence is the well-trafficked highway in and out of process, in and out of the center, in and out of the sacred's grove. Like any ancient and well-traveled highway between two capitals,

reverence can be mapped. It has its laws and principles and restrictions, just as surely as it has its destinations; and it requires its
own particular forms of maintenance to the point even of having,
like every necessary road, its own maintenance crews and verge
keepers.

But while the road holds constant, its principles and laws stable
and fixed, the variable with reverence as with any road is in its
travelers — in their vehicles, in their reasons for travel and their
expectations of it, in their vision of the route as they move along
it, and, most distinguishing, in their selective choices of what to
pack for the journey and later of what to remember and record
and assimilate from the journey once they have set out upon it.

Richness of experience for one traveler may be poverty for
another, or an equal degree of lavishness of experience may be
created for two different travelers out of very dissimilar accommodations and agenda. Bearing in mind this cordial generosity within
travel, any traveler would be wise, or so it would seem, to look
briefly at the constant before he or she begins to consider the variables. He or she would be well advised, in other words, to look
first at reverence, the road.

*   *   *   *   *

Reverence may be an attitude — it inarguably is; and it may be
a road in, a means — it surely is. But it is also, like most roads,
subject to two principles that may or may not be seen as working
to the best interests of those concerned. The answer to that one
usually depends on who is being asked from what perspective as
well as from what time frame.

First, reverence is subject to codification. *Subject* is an understatement of sorts, because reverence is downright susceptible
to codification in pretty much the same way that a first-grader
is susceptible to head colds and runny noses and with equally
unattractive results. Second, reverence, like most roads, does not
clearly cease to be at some given point or place but tends rather

to flow into one more or less continuous mesh with all of its inter-sectors and connectors. There is little need actually for it to do otherwise, nor would most of us want it to.

We would find it silly as well as laborious, for example, to have to say, every time we drove down a country road, "Aha! Here, at this exact spot, the front wheels of my car have rolled on to Ac-cess Road 127 and have left my back wheels still on Route 6. In three miles, my front wheels will turn into my mother's driveway and leave my back wheels briefly still on the access road — unless, of course, I decide to go only 1.2 miles to Pleasantville and take the turnpike north in order to come along the county maintenance road," and so on. In just the same way that a familiar network of roads can take us smoothly home for a visit, so reverence con-nects us smoothly and almost without demarcation not only with the sacred that we seek but also with various vantage points from which to both view and approach it.

Codification, on the other hand, at one and the same time, is both more obvious and less forgiving as a characteristic than is fluidity. Codification — a systemization of method; a laying down of rules and principles based on established efficacy and/or in-spired instruction; an expanded and ever-expanding accretion of test cases, of learned annotations, of conservatory opinions; a nexus of regulation with consequences. They all mean the same thing. They mean to describe a system of laws, a governance of conduct with the intent of achieving some desired result and, second, of maintaining in constant practice those principles and methods that have historically proven themselves useful for that purpose. In short and in the case of reverence particularly, they mean morality — morality with a strong overlay of ethnicity and a truly frightening potential for social enforcement, conservatory corruption, and an insupportable weightiness.

Morality is as necessary to life as reverence is, because it is reverence's flesh and bone. It just also happens to be reverence's weak spot, its Achilles' heel, the blemish on its aesthetic perfection. Were it not for morality and its entropic tendency to turn ugly — its absolute proclivity, one might say, for meanness and/or enervating tediousness — reverence would be as totally satisfying and sufficient an experience to almost all human beings as it was to the women of Saltillo. About that, Sophia and the Beatitudes are both correct. Reverence among the poor in purse and circumstance is pure reverence to the extent that it is freed from any great exercise of social choice and thereby from its own fatal corruptibility. The morality of the absolutely poor and disenfranchised is simply not worth the effort of elaborate codifying.

On an individual as well as on a class basis, the disciplines of reverence can sometimes be beautiful and sustaining adjuncts to life, of course. There can be no question about that. For instance, when discipline rests in a reverent man like Marcus Aurelius, who is relatively removed from the realities of others by elevated station, or in one like Saint Benedict, removed by private or cloistered choice, the results are so fertile that they enrich more than one lifetime. They enrich a whole culture. It is more frequently in a social, cultural, political setting that the practice of reverence can become so codified that it usurps the sacred and begins to supersede it.

The consequence, at a real-life level, is that for most Americans today reverence cannot by itself be sufficient either as a subjective experience or as an approach to the sacred. Yet paradoxically, those who seek for the sacred must have reverence — its disciplines and its codices — if ever they are to arrive at the yearned-for destination. It is a conundrum, and nothing testifies more poignantly to it than does the strong, recent, and current performance of books about reverence's physical face.

The blockbuster general (i.e., secular) sales of books like William Bennett's *The Book of Virtues,* Stephen Carter's *The Culture of Disbelief,* or former Vice-President Dan Quayle's *Standing Firm* would alone validate adult America's absorption with pure, unadulterated morality. But that is not the interesting thing about books of this type. The interesting thing is that almost none of them is "religious" as such. That is, very few of them are sectarian or proselytizing. Yet both as a genre and as specific, individual titles they have managed to command a hefty portion of their total sales and probably the heftiest part of their word-of-mouth support from religious, specialized, and/or non–general interest retail outlets like book fairs, theological, seminary, university, and Christian bookstores, and even parish and cathedral book tables. They have succeeded in grassroots, religious America just as completely as they have in college-trained, BMW America.

The consequence of too much affinity between religion and morality, especially with a morality that has lost connection with its natal reverence, is, as we all know far too well, that religion, like reverence, soon gets subsumed. And religion gone moralistic is predestined to be unattractive in any age. The alignment of organized religion with morality directly rather than in the overarching context of reverence not only diminishes the religious life but also the religion, for it denies it its communal gifts of compassion, charity, and humor. We today are bearing pained witness to that very process.

On the other hand, the balanced alignment of a moral reverence with organized religion can have much appeal, especially to those seeking theistically for the sacred. One of the most, if not the most, dynamic evidences of our current American yearning for this kind of reverential morality within the framework of an established religion is the growth of Islam among us. The fastest-growing faith in the United States, Islam is characterized by an exquisite morality — exquisite in that it is very carefully tended and pruned by what Islam calls "the practice of spiritual chivalry," the aesthetic progression of the believer from moral goodness into the state of being a friend of God. There is little question that the growth of Islam is tied directly to this emphasis on morality and upon the mechanisms for maintaining it reverentially. Even a casual study of the expanded lists of new and forthcoming books on Islam and Islamic practice in this country and of the growing number of U.S.-based Islamic publishing houses further confirms this point.[5]

For most of us, then, whether we turn to Islam or to some other form of trimming and focusing the interplay between morality and the social contract, there just must be more than reverence involved in our engagement of the sacred. Reverence as a way is good for us only if it is one part within a larger map of roads and paths — if, that is, it takes us in by way of other vistas that have richer views and greater immediacy.

Those other and ancillary ways are manifold, but they may all be categorized under one of two possibilities: spirituality or religion. Of the two, spirituality is the less likely to suffer the slings and arrows of an outrageous and outraging morality; but by the same token, spirituality with its potential for idiosyncretism and laxness can become alienating and isolating. Religion is, as we have said, almost more likely than is reverence itself to succumb fatally to moralism; but it is, by its very etymology, incorporating and connecting.

Both spirituality and religion, of course, by being merely views of, or points from which to view, the sacred, share a commonality of destination as well as certain overt characteristics. And both of them usually cohabit, in some varying, relative proportions, in the reverent human being. I have, however, seen the two totally balanced, totally coequal, once — but only once — in my life. That opportunity, which I can only describe as a kind of exposure to radiance, was so graphic and so formative for me that, though it was a relatively recent experience, I feel compelled to recount it here — to look first, in other words, at spirituality and religion in balance before we look at either of them separately.

A Recounting

S OME STORIES of the wait-till-I-tell-you-what-happened-to-
me kind are egotistical flotsam, and some are just the
natural segues of easy conversation. Some are poignant
ploys in disguise, dressed-up requests for the explication of trou-
blesome events from a sympathetic but more removed point of
view. And some of them are not really the property of their nar-
rators at all. They are not even stories in the usual sense but are
more nearly things — free-standing things — that have to be described as a solitary building in the middle of an open field must
be described, or recounted as must the impact of a great painting
or a terrible history. What follows here is a little of all of these; and
its surrounding circumstances, if they are not exactly ordinary, are
at least very straightforward.

On Saturday, May 28, 1994, a month to the day after South
Africa had completed its first free elections and Nelson Mandela
had won the presidency of his homeland, Archbishop Desmond
Tutu, his wife, and his media secretary, a white South African jour-
nalist named John Allen, flew to Los Angeles. For the Archbishop
and Allen, as for dozens of lesser luminaries, it was the beginning
of that decidedly American process known as "book promotion"
and the first, preliminary step in that related thing, "the book
tour."

They would repeat the whole process five months later in early
October when Tutu's book *The Rainbow People of God,* a col-

lection of the Archbishop's significant papers from over the years with connective essays by Allen, was actually a book in their hands. But in May, it was enough that their manuscript was finished, that the type had been set on time, and that there were readers' samplers available, complete with a full-color reproduction of *Rainbow People*'s cover on the front of each sampler.

The occasion for their coming was the annual Convention and Trade Show of the American Booksellers Association, where the future of new and forthcoming books is gauged by, and advanced orders in large part determined on the basis of, the authors' reputations, the authors' conversation about their books, and slender reader's samplers with handsome, full-color jacket reproductions on their covers. So Archbishop Tutu was in Los Angeles to address several thousand of America's more influential and accomplished booksellers as well as to socialize at small gatherings with some of its most successful ones.

The archbishop was tired, but that had been a predictable and predicted situation. He had already been on the road for almost two weeks, having left Johannesburg ahead of Allen and Mrs. Tutu to travel on church business, and then flown to Los Angeles by way of other meetings in New York. His address to the convention was scheduled for Monday morning, and the plan called for him to spend the intervening two days refreshing himself, catching up on events with his wife, and working with Allen through the correspondence and decisions that had accumulated during his absence from South Africa. The plan called also for him to observe the Sabbath quietly in his hotel suite, where he would celebrate the Eucharist with his own party and a few guests.

We guests were seven in number, making, with Mrs. Tutu, Allen, and the archbishop, ten of us gathered on that Sunday morning in May in the living room of a tenth-floor suite in the downtown Los Angeles Hyatt: the archbishop's American editor and college-sophomore daughter, an assistant editor, the archbishop's agent and her husband, the religion products buyer from one of the country's largest bookstore chains and a dear friend of mine, and I.

We were all there as devout Christians. That was the first thing that struck me as I entered that shadowy, generic room. I, like all of them, had been invited several days beforehand by phone, and I had been blatantly flattered. No reaction, I quickly realized, could have been more inappropriate or more out of touch with the reality before me. Whoever each of us was outside that hotel door in the world of books and intellectual politics was not enough to have gotten any one of us through it, nor was position the basis of our assembling.

We had been summoned as a community of worshippers, and the reason for our being there was singular, not various. Each of us was indeed an influential book professional and for that reason in Los Angeles at the time; but aside from that selective happenstance, the reason was our shared Christianity.

To enter that badly lighted, long-nosed room with its pseudo personal furniture and its glass-topped everything, was, as nothing in my life had ever been before, to enter the imagined catacombs of Christian history. Admittedly, there had been a suggestive cachet of surreptitiousness about the whole thing right from the beginning, a pleasant furtiveness about how we had been directed to assemble in such a way as to protect Archbishop Tutu for as long as possible from any public engagement. Yet when my friend and I knocked on the hall door and were admitted, there was more than the exhilaration of some sweet secrecy already operative in that room.

People whom we did not know and who apparently had not previously known each other were talking among themselves, making introductions and small talk as people upon meeting will. But a part of their individual attentions had already moved to the purpose of our coming. It was obvious in the stillness of their hands, in how they kept them in their laps or to their sides. It showed in the way their eyes drifted sometimes away from the faces and toward the surroundings, seeing nothing. It showed most in their soft, uninquiring conversation.

When we arrived, the archbishop, wearing a black and aqua-blocked nylon jogging suit and white Nikes, was already seated in front of the double windows at the far end of the room in one of the place's two high-backed chairs. To his right was an octagonal lamp table and beyond that the other and matching, high-backed chair, still empty. To his left was another table — the low, square kind that hotels put in corners to fill up the incongruities between overstuffed low sofas and overstuffed high-backed chairs.

As if to thwart the Hyatt's decorative intentions, John Allen, in khakis and a white shirt whose sleeves he had long since rolled up over his elbows, had judiciously placed a straight-backed desk chair in front of the corner table. He was sitting there now, or rather he was perched upon the edge of it now, his arms and legs all crossed upon themselves and his angular attention clearly focused on someone or something he was expecting.

To Allen's left and sitting on the sofa itself was Mrs. Tutu, as relaxed and nested-in as Allen seemed restive and perched. A coffee table that, guessing by the depressions in the rug, had originally stood in front of the sofa had been pulled up toward the archbishop and was now within easy reach both of his chair and Allen's. Three or four copies of the Scriptures were already on the table and three or four copies of what I discovered later was the South African edition of the Book of Common Prayer.

Running almost the entire length of the other interior wall was a library table that had been anchored in place by a massive arrangement of dried flowers and in front of which someone had arranged four more desk chairs. To our left as my friend and I came in, and more or less blocking the passageway into the bed- and bathrooms, were three or four folding chairs pulled into place so that they faced the windows, the coffee table altar, and the archbishop.

"Please," he said in that singularly lilting speech of the native

South African when he speaks English. "Please be seated with us. We are waiting just now for the bread to come up from room service."

Had the Archbishop of the Anglican Church of South Africa danced naked in front of me I would not have been more taken aback, nor could I have been any more efficiently and quickly thrust into the attitudes of his reverence. To be waiting for a bell-man to bring up bread from the kitchen was so matter-of-fact, so unpretentiously reasonable as to be the act only of a humble man. The Bread of Christ from the kitchens of Hyatt. I could never have done such a thing — which, I understood immediately, was a limitation in some dark way akin to the self-inflation that had allowed me to be flattered by all of this in the first place.

While we waited, the Archbishop made bits of small talk, but most of the time he deferred to Mrs. Tutu, who chatted with the room in general about her flight, the elections, her predictions for the Mandela presidency, and the state of her children. The knock came within no more than five minutes, and a young face peered around the door, proffering a small plate with two naked slices of light bread uncovered and drying on it.

"You want this, sir?" the boy said, his amazement that he'd been sent upstairs on so unorthodox a mission as obvious as his confusion about why there were ten, seemingly sober people waiting for him to accomplish it. To the day of my death I will be willing to wager good money that that young man had no idea to whom he was delivering two slices of untoasted sandwich bread or why, but I would wager the same money that he has not yet forgotten the fact that he did it.

"Thank you, I'll take it," said Allen, across the room before anyone else to take the plate and pay the tip. Making his way more deliberately back through the obstructing chairs, Allen pulled the coffee table a bit closer to Archbishop Tutu, set the plate down upon it, and resumed his own seat. He reached under the lamp table, took out his briefcase from beneath it, and from the briefcase took out a small, airline-sized bottle of Glen Ellen wine that he had obviously bought on the plane during his flight. He set the bottle beside the bread and replaced the briefcase under the table. All the necessary parts of the richly imagistic Christian mass were in place.

"Good," said the Archbishop. "Now we shall begin." And he started assigning our roles. To Allen the job of leading the Prayers of the People, to me the reading of the Old Testament Lesson, to his editor's daughter the Epistle. So be it. Next he spoke the prayers of consecration over the elements in a voice so low I could not distinguish the words, but in which I thought I heard the occasional clicking sounds of his native tongue.

"Blessed be God: Father, Son, and Holy Ghost," he said, lifting his head and addressing us in English, and we responded in kind, "And blessed be his kingdom, now and for ever. Amen." The opening prayers were said, the Gloria recited, the Kyrie spoken; and long before even that much was done, I, like everyone else in that room, had already slipped effortlessly into the habits of a lifetime, walking once more without self-awareness or any awareness at all along the familiar road into the center.

The Old Testament Lesson and the Epistle were read and then, as celebrant, the Archbishop read the Gospel, rendering it mellifluous and rhythmic with the rise and fall of his almost-familiar English. The readings finished, he turned to us and said, "It is Trinity Sunday, the first in the freedom of my people, and I am pleased to observe it here with you."

Trinity Sunday — the Sunday after Pentecost — both celebrates the triune God and opens the longest of Christianity's liturgical seasons. It is a major feast day for many parts of Christendom. "We celebrate the three parties of God," he was saying, "the community of God as the Father, and God as the Son, and God as the Holy Spirit."

It was the voice carrying me now, the modulations, the simplicity, the pastoral intimacy of it. "Father, Son, and Holy Ghost, God is a society and we are created in his image. The idea of a single human being is therefore a contradiction," and he began, in the soft persuasive litany of his melodic speech, to weave the spell of our common sonship. As he spoke, I slipped farther and farther into an understanding that was so clear to him as to become transparent through him. What I employed as a religious principle and a moral convention, he was.

Then the homily was over as unceremoniously as it had begun, with his turning simply to the words of the Nicene Creed: "I believe in one God...." We repeated with him the time-hallowed tenets of our faith and then waited as Allen took up the Prayers of the People.

If I had experienced the spirit of the priest in Tutu, I had at least been prepared to some greater or lesser extent by his position and his episcopacy. I had had no such prior warning about John Allen. Instead, it was the priesthood of all believers that rolled out of him, filling that room and us gathered there in it with all the urgency and poignancy of primal belief. He prayed as one talks to the landlord, he prayed as one talks to his daddy, he prayed as one talks to the suffering, he prayed as one talks to a lover, he prayed as I have never heard prayer before, and Mrs. Tutu prayed with him, filling his pauses and breaks and silences with petitions of her own for her country, her family, her husband, her faith and constancy, her friends; and punctuating them both the voice of the archbishop, sometimes in English, sometimes clearly now in his native tongue. The three of them rose and swelled and peaked and receded and rose again like an ocean calm before its own strength, and there was no doubt among them, no hesitancy, no modesty. They were as one body somewhere where we could still see them and almost go, praying with expectancy and absolute surety. But these three were no chimneys to the light. These were its lamps in consultation together with God himself to shape the world, and they were being burned by the light. They were, in fact, luminous with it.

I had understood reverence from young adulthood. I had understood access to the sacred for almost as many years, and religion as an expression of it. I had even understood spirituality, if by that one means that I had myself lived within and through the practices of spirituality, and I had recognized its effects both in myself and in others; but I had never before sat and watched it being enacted by human bodies in rational and clearly not ecstatic commerce with the sacred, using the body's tongue and the body's concerns.

The effect, however — the luminosity and transparent sighting into a palpable glory — I had seen only once before, in Gallery 6 of the National Gallery of Art. The *Ginevra de' Benci* hangs there, the only painting in this country by Leonardo da Vinci. Ignorant of its presence, I went wandering one hot day several summers ago through the museum, more cooling than looking, when I rounded a corner into Gallery 6 and was sucked violently and physically into her transparency.

What lay beyond the figure of Ginevra was the naked, exposed, untamed domain of the spirit — terrible in its beauty, terrible in its perfection, terrible in how it fulfilled me in itself and left me without myself. Ineffable in glory, luminous in light. What I had seen was the imagination.

What I had seen before the *Ginevra* and was seeing again around a jerry-rigged altar in the Los Angeles Hyatt, I realized almost immediately, was just that — the imagination. It was not whether or not John Allen and Desmond Tutu were praying any more than it was a matter of whether Leonardo had been painting. The thing that was happening was the imaging. Twice in my life now, while I watched, some human being or other had stood in the portal between the world of the spirit and the world of the flesh and held the curtain aside so that, fully in the body, I fully saw.

All those sins of stupidity and human pride that had for a lifetime made me hear "imagination" with the prejudiced ears that translated it to "weak tool of childish intellect," "suspect recourse of the gullible," "insubstantial evidence born of human projection" — all of those came tumbling down around me. All of them are true, of course. All of them are true until one has seen beyond their hearing. Then that which has been understood becomes the valid.

What happened after that — the celebration of the mass itself, the final blessing and dismissal, the more secular good-byes — they all happened and in their proper sequence. My friend and I left as we had come, together; and though we have made mention of that morning on several occasions since, we have found each time that there is nothing to say *about* what we saw. In the final analysis it seems to be, as I said in the beginning, possible only to recount it.

– 7 –

What the Means and Gifts of Spirituality Are

I HAD A MIDDLE-AGED, THOROUGHLY AGNOSTIC FRIEND several years ago who verged at times on being an outright if somewhat low-key and nonmilitant atheist. He was fond of saying that spirituality is "like heaven naked, but with an attitude." My friend had one of the richest spiritual lives I have ever witnessed, a fact that no doubt lent some considerable weight in my mind to what he was saying. Even allowing for that, however, I would still hold, I think, that his definition of spirituality is as fine a one as I have ever heard and a better one than I probably could ever invent.

His were also the first definition and life — for they can never really be disentwined, can they? — to reveal to me so graphically the discreteness of religion and spirituality as entities. The fact that the two are complementary in the lives of most of us had always blinded me to the distinctiveness of each. My friend's ability to live that distinction gracefully and richly was a great gift to me. By seeing spirituality as he saw and lived it, separate from all theisms, I came also to a more elegant and economical spirituality — or if not that, then to at least a recognition that such was possible within the nature of spirituality. Any limitations upon spirituality came more from my own impoverishment of daring, in other words, than from some inherent restriction in it.

Spirituality, seen naked of God, is a place of unknowing:[1] the domain of the soul where image is as language is to the body within the physical world and where a glowing presentness is as the body is in the world of human affairs; where silence is musical and light without source is everywhere in the numen; where instruction comes without words and slips in as revelation; where forces flow so powerfully and in so foreign a coursing that, coming to the window of consciousness in order all the better to see them, the mind must name them instead, calling them like phantasmagoria by their roles and not their essence — spirits, angels, demons, and devils; where, timeless and boneless, every reconfiguring soul wanders in communion with what is, and wisdom is as logic is to mind.

Spirituality is not, like reverence, an attitude, an intention of the mind, though the mind may yearn for it, and the mind may, in extremis, become the soul's last cry and final spokesman. But my friend was right; spirituality *has* an attitude. It has an edge, a rigor, an economy, and a governance of its own that can be neither changed nor circumvented. They are its texture, the scheme of its being, and the armed guardians of its integrity and its borders. They are the soul's constitution, its canon of being, and its principles of operation whether under God or simply within the poor, dumb creature, the creature who can no more escape soul than he or she can escape body. Like the tree of life to the ancients, the menorah of first tradition, humankind has roots and trunks and heaven-stretching, light-seeking, sap-holding, seed-bearing, wind-knowing limbs. We have soul and body and spirit.[2] One union in three parts until....

* * * * *

The gifts of the body to Life are logic and procreation. The contributions of the soul are wisdom and, somewhat ironically, incorporation. And by the grace either of God or the Tao, according to one's point of reference, neither will allow the other to become dominant nor itself to be forgotten. Much of present American spirituality, much of the incredible, almost unprecedented, dramatic, historic — stack all the adjectival hyperbole you want and we will not yet have overstated the present matter — much of the foment about spirituality going on in America today, particularly among our baby boomer generation, is a righting up of that balance, a corrective readjustment. Over two hundred years of Enlightenment have fed logic too well, making it fat and sluggish and more than a little dyspeptic. Logic is letting its displeasure be known by mooning us with the backside of its limitations. At the same time, lean souls, like Pharaoh's seven starved cows, are eating up our resources in psychiatrists' fees, medical bills, addiction center charges, police support taxes, and a thousand other debilitating drains upon the goodness of the body's life.

There surely can be no mystery about why a book titled *Care of the Soul* would stay on the *New York Times* bestseller list for forty-two weeks in 1992 and still be on the religion/spirituality bestseller lists even as I am writing this. Thomas Moore opens that book by saying:

> The great malady of the 20th century, implicated in all our troubles and affecting us individually and socially, is "loss of soul." When the soul is neglected, it doesn't go away; it appears symptomatically in obsessions, addictions, violence and loss of meaning.[3]

And from that opening position, Moore goes on to create an elegant manual for soul care as well as two subsequent volumes that have likewise found insatiable audiences and apparently inexhaustible markets — Americans, desperate in their bodies to achieve again intercourse with their souls.

Intercourse is of course the ancient metaphor for the dance of the body and the soul, of logic and wisdom. As the tree was to our ancestors the symbol of their indivisible union, so human preening, caressing, courting, and seducing were the metaphor for the cohabitation of their parts.

It was said by the ancients that even god(s) had a soul, despite my wise and spiritual friend's notions to the contrary. Among the Hebrews, from whose roots Islam, Judaism, and Christianity all draw their informing, mythic past, God's soul was female, the beautiful woman of the clearing. She was female and he knew her as we know her — as wisdom. She was present with him in creation, and with him shaped it and us like him/them in that image and by that pattern. Her name is Sophia.

While Rosie and Johnny and 98 percent of their friends probably never heard of Sophia and would have been repelled as by idolatry if they ever had, the truth is that Sophia has, in the last three or four years, become a very, very visible face on the shelves of bookstores and her name a very, very familiar one in the mouths and newspapers of Johnny's great-grandchildren. Usually represented by a symbol or depicted by a reproduction of the sculpted head of a Greek goddess, Sophia has opened up a whole new world to theists weary of masculine, hierarchical (i.e., logical) God; to feminists politically weary of the same thing, both in the flesh and in the spirit; to the reverent who recognize her as the lady of the sacred; to the shrewd who acknowledge her obvious benefits; to the neopagan who would live within her powers; and to the blatantly blasphemous who would prostitute her as goddess to their iconoclasm.

The range is so broad, the spectrum of possibilities so poorly segmented and marked, that her very name now titillates.[4] But above and beneath all the furor, the metaphor still holds. The soul will be loved and will love through a process and toward a union that is as human love is in its process and culminating union. The soul must be courted by the mind in order that she may ease, comfort, fulfill, and glorify the mind, releasing it and herself into an ecstasy of spirit beyond them both.

*   *   *   *   *

The soul is courted, as any woman is, by a tender knowledge of her private parts and her pleasures and, if courted correctly, with a certain hesitant foreboding about her consuming cruelties. Short of rape itself, soul is mistress of the game; and accepting in order that she may borrow into herself is her role within the courtship dance. Logic, like any man, enters at his peril if he does not enter subject to the rules that appertain.

And whether we consciously think nowadays of our soul's life in so sexual a way as did our ancient forebears, we still, as if by a genetic encoding, function as if we do. Spirituality and the courting of the soul and the carrying off of her wisdom are, first and foremost, acts of the mind's self-denial, its willful and willing subjection of itself in order to lose the awareness. To have intercourse with the soul, the consciousness must be freed to travel into her chambers;[5] and how we do that today is very much as men and women have always done it, save that now we have to work in every activity of our lives at freeing the consciousness to travel and now we write thousands of books about how to accomplish that — books on spirituality in general and on meditation, centering, dailiness and sacramentalizing, and the like, in particular — about two thousand such books within the last year alone, by my best estimate.

That river of books that seems presently to be at floodtide had its beginnings in the small press and underground publications — many of them quite literally done on a kitchen table — of the New Age movement; for whatever else New Age is and becomes, it was originally the first loud cry of the abandoned and starving soul. And from those early volumes to the bestselling manuals by Richard Foster on spiritual formation[6] to the plethora of Zen manuals both about and not about motorcycles to *A Course in Miracles*[7] and Marianne Williamson's *Return to Love*[8] to Thomas Moore to the deluge of two thousand such books a year in an unbroken progression, the bulk of it is composed of volumes that by whatever name or method or out of whatever tradition still are courting handbooks. Submission to the beloved, listening to the beloved with understanding, touching the beloved with a sweet impatience that does not wish to hurry — these are the postures and necessary attitudes; and they all require a prior stilling of the mind, a centering of it back into its own sphere of natural being and realm of influence.

The mind must separate itself from the awareness. It must be firmly within the body and not upon its parapets or riding the beams of its own projections; and the body in which mind governs must be well-tended and calm around it. In earlier times, or so we like to imagine, there were fewer parapets and less time for projections, a more natural centeredness of the mind; and there is probably no small element of truth in that nostalgic notion.

"Who bakes the bread bakes more than the stomach's food," says the old proverb, and the truth contained in those words is indeed one of the great truths of the human experience. It can be applied likewise, of course, to the weaving of cloth, the growing of flowers[9] and/or one's own food, the building of one's own house — to any of those activities, necessary to the physical life, that can be and are accomplished by having the user and the maker be one and the same. Such a lifestyle is the ultimate and most unforgiving of tethers, but it is beneficial to the courting awareness. Bereft now of such naturally occurring confinements, we postmoderns must study to show ourselves approved as suitors.

When the hands are occupied and the mind stilled by the routinized, the monotonous, the diurnal, then the awareness slips across the barrier and dances with the soul's images. Surrounded by them, awash and at sea in them, suspended, caressed, supported, the attention slumbers awake on the soul's bosom, lulled to fullness and contented as by a mother's hand, while some sustaining mystery persuades it.

The mystery, of course, will not travel back to mind with the attention, but sometimes fragments of its images and patterns will, as in the *Ginevra* or any other great work of art.[10] Then we, in all our intelligences, in our body as well as our soul, recognize them as beloved familiars; and in those minutes of recognition (which we call by the name of magic), we briefly know the union of ourselves, the harmonious totality of all our parts. That glory, like the perfect orgasm, we can neither speak nor forget. We can only recount to one another like some ancient mariner our engagement of it.

And sometimes, as with Desmond Tutu, some few among us can move without investment into the mysterium and reveal it by association as one reveals the bedroom in dining room conversation. But always, the fruits of spirituality and its union evidence themselves in the life lived — in its contextualized serenity even when it is invaded by anxiety, in its disciplined and reasoned accomplishment even when it knows itself to be less than fully accomplished, in its compassion and generous expenditures, in its wisdom.

* * * * *

"I looked into the eye of the newt," says the haiku, "and saw Fujiyama behind me."[11] It is the observation of a wise man and is itself a piece of wisdom; but it is also the stating of a principle. In the particular — the very small and isolated particular — the wisely directed attention can always discover the whole that resides there. The mystery in its smallest dimensions is the mystery in its largest ones, for the mysterium has no substance with which to occupy space or time. Like the sacred whose agent and proof text it is, the mysterium is.

Which is why my agnostic friend so enriched me and why I continue to hold his observation of heaven naked as a great gift. There is in presentness less than enough. There is no story; and story is the work of religion.

— Interlude —

A Story

TO TELL THIS STORY, I must tell a story about the story. I have always suspected that there are things, even in the earliest stages of our lives, that as we express it usually, "seem to speak to us," people or events or stories that haunt us, ones for which we seem to have some kind of natural or ordained affinity. These events or people or tales become almost prophetic, as if their properties and distinguishing characteristics in some way resonated with an intricate, hidden pattern within ourselves or our destiny — as if like were meeting like. The story I am about to tell was that for me. It is, for that reason, a classic example of what I have come to call a totem story; that is, it defines me, and I intuitively recognize it as the original pattern up out of which my own life is one applied variation.

It began when I was a child — the only child of a gracious and brilliant academic and an equally brilliant, fairly daring flapper-turned-devoted-wife to a man ten years her senior. Having come late in a marriage that was already tardy, at least for my father, I arrived as sole inheritor of all her experience and his knowledge. It was an interesting place to be and mine an interesting childhood.

One of the understood habits of our days was that I was instructed during the day, but in the evenings I was exposed to the soul's converse: to the arts, to music, to good drama, and to that mainstay of postdepression American homes, the evening story-time. My father read aloud as some men paint or sculpt and with

the same passions toward perfection in delivery, shading, and nu-
ance. He was at this one thing above all others a consummate
artist. The choice of what was read, however, was mine to make,
within reason, meaning the same story no more than twice in any
one week. What that meant was that on at least two nights of
every week of the last five of my first eight years I heard, read
aloud from *Hurlburt's Book of Bible Stories For Children,* "The
Story."

"The Story" is certainly familiar enough to many Americans,
but it bears repeating here, at least briefly. Laying aside the flour-
ishes and subtleties with which my father delivered it, the story,
stripped down and lean, is simple.

In the thirty-seventh year of the Exodus, the tribes of Israel
came to rest once more in the Sinai desert. It had now been almost forty years since the original Children of Israel, the men and
women who had known slavery and oppression in Egypt, had followed a man called Moses out into the desert; forty years since
those who had felt the lash and known the shame had also known
the glory of seeing the Red Sea part to let them through and the
glory of Pharaoh's drowning; forty years since they had trekked
with their herds and their stolen Egyptian jewelry and their little ones across the Sinai Peninsula and come at last to the very
borders of the Promised Land that flowed with milk and honey;
forty years since they had sent twelve spies, one from each of their
tribes, across those borders to spy out the land before they moved
to attack and take it; forty years since the fateful consequence of
that sad day.

With the dust of Egypt still upon them, the escaping Children
of Israel had, under Moses' leadership, moved quickly from the
northern borders of Egypt to the western ones of Canaan. With
dispatch they had appointed their spies, each tribe selecting a wise
as well as an astute man; and then they had waited across Jordan on the eastern side for the spies to return. For forty days they
waited in the camps, and for forty days the twelve spies searched

out the land across Jordan. But when they did at last return, they brought with them both samples of the produce of the land and frightening words.

The land, they said, was inhabited by giants too large, too organized, and too well armed for the untrained clans of Israel. To attack would be death. Surely Moses had misunderstood or Yahweh had changed his intent for them. The situation was without remedy and the Children of Israel must withdraw from Jordan's banks, not crossing it but traveling below its fords and finding another place through which to enter, or even another land.

Of the twelve, two spies, Joshua and Caleb, disagreed, protesting that the hand of Yahweh was greater than the hands of men. What Yahweh had promised, he would deliver. They must move forward or risk apostasy and disobedience. As always, though, the voice of ten superseded the counsel of two. The Children of Israel refused to follow Moses into Canaan and turned south instead.

Then it was that God spoke to Moses and through him to the Children. Because of this rebellious act of distrust and defiance, the Children would wander homeless in the wilderness for forty years, one year for each day that their spies had searched out the Promised Land. They would wander until every man and woman who had known Pharaoh's hand was dead, buried in the shallow sands of the merciless desert. Only when those who had not known that curse of slavery were adult in Israel, only when those who had not seen the Angel of Death pass over Egypt's homes or the Red Sea part had grown up to become Israel, only then would Yahweh fulfill his promise to a new generation. He would begin again with the Children's children, taking them safely to the land promised to Abraham, Isaac, and Jacob.

Now it was the thirty-seventh year of their pilgrimage through waterless places and purposeless tracks of sand, and the time of deliverance was approaching. Those who wandered now had grown up in the desert and had left behind them in its shallow graves and half-scooped caves the parents and grandparents who had been apostate. It was the Children's children who came in those fateful weeks to gather one last time at the foot of Mount Horeb and wait out the remaining months in its shadow. But as one day led purposelessly to another and that day to a third, the Children's children, weary of too much wandering and too little accomplishment, themselves rebelled as had their forebears.

Protesting to Moses that Yahweh was no longer interested in them or their plight, that the desert was hard and the tales of life in Egypt nostalgically sweet, they like their fathers and mothers before them tempted God's anger. And there came among them there in the camps huge snakes, serpents such as live in the desert. And the snakes came in in droves, so that there were serpents in the manna baskets and serpents in the bedrolls and serpents in the babies' hammocks. Everywhere serpents and everywhere men and women and children screaming out their terror and their pain — and their ending, for the snakes were killing the people.

Hearing the cries, Moses went running out into the camp; and seeing him, the Children's children cried out, "We have sinned. Implore Yahweh for mercy. Help us, help us."

Moses, the story says, went quickly to the Tent of Meeting to implore God's deliverance for his repentant people. God, for his part accepting their cries of sorrow as an offering of repentance, told Moses to fashion from the bronze braziers of the sanctuary a serpent in every way like those that were afflicting and killing the people. He was then to take the serpent he had made, place it upon a cross pole with its body twined in the way of snakes around the crosspiece, and march through the camp of Israel with the serpent-draped pole held high before him. Whoever looked up at the bronze serpent, Yahweh said, would be saved from death — *not from being bitten,* but from death as a result of being bitten.

Moses, doing as he had been told, quickly hammered a brazier into a serpent, entwined it upon a cross pole, and went through the corridors of tents crying, "Look up, look up." Those men and women and children who believed him and believed in Yahweh's message through him, looked up at the cross pole with its burnished snake and not down at the desert vipers that were besieging them. They elected by a combined act of will and faith to look, not down where the agony was and where the snakes might still be pulled from their bodies and their children's bodies, but up where the mercy was promised. They elected to be bitten in order that by faith they might live. And, the story says, some eighteen months later those who made that choice entered by way of Jericho and its tumbling walls into the Promised Land, the land flowing with milk and honey.

It is a horrendous story, complete with all the elements that fire a child's imagination. It totally absorbed me and mine for years (and still does; I find it the most significant story in the Old Testament, as a matter of fact). It totally absorbed me for years before I went to college and discovered in anthropology classes about sympathetic medicine and sympathetic shamanism; about how using the thing that is afflicting in order to cure the affliction is one of humanity's oldest understandings. I was intellectually fascinated by that association, but no more than that, and certainly in no way diverted by it from an adoring respect for the story.

For one thing, by the time I hit sympathetic shamanism, I had already hit several other, far more significant things. I had lived long enough to know for a hard, enduring fact that life is full of snakes, that they bite fiercely, that they will kill if you look down and wrestle them, that being wrestled with somehow gives them the potency with which to kill, and that looking up doesn't stop the pain immediately but it does prevent death from it. I had learned to look at a score of things by the time I hit anthropology class and to say to each of them, "You're a snake," and know I was speaking the truth.

I had also made another discovery. The best-loved Bible verse among my contemporaries — and I suspect even among Americans now — is John 3:16: "For God so loved the world, that he gave his only begotten Son, that whosoever believeth in him should not perish, but have everlasting life." The curious thing is that we rarely, if ever, read or speak the opening few lines of that famous quotation.

Christ is speaking to his disciples and, as Saint John records the words in verses 14, 15, and 16, what Christ says is: "And as Moses lifted up the serpent in the wilderness, even so must the Son of man be lifted up: That whosoever believeth in him should not perish, but have eternal life. For God so loved the world," and so on.

It is one of only a very few times when the Christ even mentions an Old Testament story at all in his teaching and one of the even fewer times when he likens himself or his actions to any of their antecedents. By the time I had chewed awhile on this wonderment, I had also discovered that the snake of the Sinai was called in Hebrew by the same word as the snake of Eden. A sobering connection.

I had also discovered that Moses' bronze snake had been taken by the Israelites into Canaan with them in their conquest of the land and that they had there begun to worship it. One of the righteous acts of good King Hezekiah when he ascended to the throne of Judah in the eighth century B.C.E. was to "break into fine pieces" Moses' snake. I had further discovered in the books of the early Christian church Saint Paul's instruction to the Corinthians to "tempt not the spirit of Christ as some of our fathers did and were destroyed of serpents."

What I had discovered, in other words, was religion — messy, sometimes repugnant, always earthy, constantly greater than morality, religion. Or I had discovered a piece of it, an example of it that worked for me.

I had a story, experientially validated, that exposed an intentional pattern, a series of planned connections operative within all of life's colorful and dreadful realities, and that established a reasonable hope of there being some merciful resolutions to them.

Reverence may be the road to the sacred, and wisdom the song of the soul in its travels to see it, but story let all of me come. Story is icon to the mystery and monstrance to the sacred just as surely as it is the text of God and the disciplinarian of religion.

– 8 –

Where Religion Comes In

ELIGION AS A WORD is born of two Latin parts: *re*, meaning "together" or "again," and *ligo, ligare,* meaning "to tie," as in our common usage of *ligature, ligament,* and so forth; thus, by pure etymology, the concept of "tying together."

In general I am always suspicious of those who begin discussions of any sort by deferring to the dictionary. Even in the best of circumstances, there is a kind of intellectual naiveté in assuming that so fluid a thing as language can have its pieces and parts captured in a printed listing anyway. Their histories, yes; their contemporary vividness, never. But religion is by its very nature a conservatory exercise and, in this case at least, *religion* has not fallen far from the parental tree. Both the word and the phenomenon are still best defined as a "tying together."[1]

There is (or so I was told as a child, though I have never since been able to validate it in printed form) an old Talmudic story about Moses and God and a conversation they had one day in the desert of Sinai. Moses, according to the story, was once more tired unto death of the Children of Israel and all their conniving, rebellious, disobedient, nonobservant, and totally human ways. In his defense, Moses was probably legitimately frustrated, but the legend presents him as whiny. It has him complaining to God in a long litany of accusations and condemnations.

The Children would not keep the camp as ritually clean as they were supposed to. There were a thousand infractions every single day. The Children would not stop talking to foreigners and aliens whose herds and caravans passed them in the desert. The Children and worst of all the Children's children simply did not show the proper respect to the Levites. They insisted on treating them as ordinary citizens just like they treated one another. The Children were derelict about forcing their children to be silent around the elders of the camp. The Children...

It went on and on and on until, the story says, there came a great weary Voice from the cloud resting above the Tent of Meeting. And the Voice said, "Moses, Moses, the trouble is that you're just more religious than I am."

Which, whether it is really a piece of Talmudic lore or not, is still a very funny story. We laugh at it because of the pungent truth it contains and because of the deftness with which it exposes the great ironies of religion.

So long as religion ties together the experiences of life into some kind of purpose and then disciplines the actions of living toward that pattern, it will still be religion. It will be religion, in other words, regardless of whether or not it even mentions God or engages God as a principle. Moreover, so long as religion is a tying together of past and present experience with future events and choices, it invites — almost presupposes, in fact — human elaboration and human contamination even if and when it does engage God. God, in other words, is neither necessary to religion nor any guarantee against its corruption.

Like it or not, Marx was right on when he characterized religion as the opiate of the people. The fallacy of his observation lies only in its predicate: that religion *can be* — or even, religion *often is* — the opiate of the people is a very accurate assessment. And religion in this country is certainly no different in all of its susceptibilities, weaknesses, and foibles from religion in any other place or time. The only exception, as we have already noted several times, is that religion in America is religion in the world's most religious nation. It is also, to all intents and purposes, almost totally theistic.[2]

Religion in America, then, is a matter of God and almost entirely a matter of the monotheistic God with whom Moses may or may not have had that apocryphal desert chat. To speak about religion here and now, therefore, is to have to speak almost exclusively in terms of the God of Abraham, Isaac, and Jacob and of the theologies, dogmas, and praxes that have evolved from that fertile beginning. It is also — and far more diagnostically in terms of our present circumstances — to have to acknowledge the fact that up until the last thirty or forty years of the American experience, God and the sacred were always one and the same thing in the general perception.

*   *   *   *   *

God, in other words, was the sacred in traditional America, but He was also thereby limited to it. Holding the two as interchangeable, at least at the effectual level of popular practice, meant that the sacred was God rather than an expressive principle of him or of his intention. It also meant an almost overweening vulnerability (as does naiveté in most situations) to eventual and essentially unavoidable confusion.

The questions, when they finally did begin to come, had been predestined to insinuate themselves into every soft spot in America's spiritual and religious immaturity — questions about the nature of worship, the function of praise, the place of the imagination, the pantheon of agencies, and so forth. The years from 1945 to 1995 were indeed ones of an enforced coming of religious age in America. The old verities would all be tested, and many of them would fail.

The discovery, then, by default and as a result of all the cultural circumstances that have besieged our recent times that the sacred can be recognized nontheistically was a great shock to our aggregate sense of things. The discovery that the soul can be well tended and well contented by engaging the sacred spiritually and only spiritually was a second great insult to America's subjective sensibilities (and for many millions of us an individually painful and threatening affront as well, inviting a reactive religiosity[3] that is only just now beginning to wane).

But perhaps the unkindest cut of all was born out of just sheer information, the exponential growth of pure, baldfaced, irrefutable facts about cultures and peoples other than and/or prior to ourselves. The forced realization that the sacred tends to be constant in all human experience whereas the experience of God tends to be doctrinally configured and therefore dogma-specific was almost the capping blow, in fact. It was a blow rendered nearly insupportable not only by what it itself said — though that was bad enough — but also by its logical sequelae.

Logically, if the sacred is found to be more or less constant whereas human engagements of God are determined to be almost everywhere and always inconsistent with one another and even incompatible; and logically, if one at the same time holds the view that God and the sacred are one and the same thing, then one or both of two conclusions must follow.

The first option is to contend that God himself must actually be the same somewhere down under all the variousnesses in humanity's religious representations of him and therefore equally accessible ultimately by means of any and all reverent religious methodologies (Universalism).

The second and very complementary option is to conclude that religion is far more suspect and much less trustworthy than is spirituality as a means of knowing Truth and Life. That is, the very inconstancy with which various religions and the various sects within every religion envision and approach the God/sacred unity makes their various schemata useless or incredible at an individual level.

While religion may have enormous cultural and social utility (and it does for most adult Americans), it is best reserved as a corporate thing, in other words. The individual, however, under this option, is best served in every part of his or her subjective experience by that which we have come to recognize and can validate as consistently and universally real for people (spirituality).

The individual is also best served — or perhaps just simply most comforted and therefore most persuaded — by that which he or she can "feel," as we have already noted in our earlier discussion of spirituality as a means of relating to the sacred. There is another, added dimension, however.

Generally the "feeling" sought (or felt) in spirituality practice is described as "health," "wellness," "balance," "peace," "mindfulness," and so forth. There is a veritable horde of such words, all of them depending from some vaguely defined but very, very real and emotionally credible sense of well-being that ties together our outside and our inside experiences — that *ties together,* that in other words is a customized, often idiosyncratic, but deeply satisfying "religion" in the oldest and most cordial sense of that word, especially when it is practiced in community. It is also a "religion" that most present-day Americans would prefer to describe by means of almost any other term. *Religion* in the American popular mind is still that other thing, that thing with doors and windows, clergy and tax-exempt status, moral expectations and social implications.

The only way out of such a conundrum as this one between Universalism and our rather distinctive American spirituality (i.e., one which is markedly practical and very applied) is either to accept it and make a choice between its possibilities or to begin to pry God and the sacred apart from one another. Neither is an easy course, and the former is certainly less stylish than the latter as well as less admirable in the popular mind. Yet in a religious culture the third option, that of simply ignoring the whole thing, is no option.

As a result of these givens, tensions, and contradictions, American religion has indeed struggled not a little over the last thirty years to steady itself. Simply to say so and leave the matter there, however, is litotes at its worst, a truly egregious understatement. Not since the Pilgrim Fathers and their imposed exile to new and hostile shores has there been so generalized a religious angst in this country or have so many individual lives been shaped by the throes of one. Yet, as is the way of humanity, we seem within the last year or two suddenly to have gained enough time and distance to at last begin to read our present in terms of our immediate past, to do so with greater calm, and to project with much less agitation our immediate future.

* * * * *

The first and most visible expression of formidable shifts in America's subjective realities and of our late-twentieth-century attempts to deal effectively with them was perhaps the New Age itself. And with the New Age, as with all the other inspirational/religious/spiritual trends we have looked at, published product is once again a sound and objective first index to the potency of a basically subjective phenomenon. We can gauge the power and influence of the New Age by looking not just at what has been and is being produced by the movement itself for itself but also at what out of it was and is supported, paid for, and presumably read by an adult American public. And the facts are that for thirty years the New Age movement has spawned and continues to spawn hundreds upon hundreds of books that sell across a broad spectrum of outlets and audiences.

If one were to characterize this outpouring, one would have to say that it has tended more toward spirituality than toward Universalism but has embraced both; that it has drawn its impetus, its audience, and certainly its rhetoric from the vocabulary and concerns of wellness; that it has opened up for the first time in this country the dark or mystical side of religion to popular consideration by dealing directly and unrestrainedly with the agencies and powers of the intangible world; and that it has been until very recently shy of presenting itself as anything other than a rebellion by the broken and still-healing against the tyranny of misinformation, rationalism, and institutionalism. The fact that the New Age has lived to grow beyond this last, self-imposed modesty is the most credible witness of all to its historic necessity and its legitimacy as a part of our own maturation as a people.

By 1987, a whole segment of America's publishing industry that did not even exist in 1965 and that is now composed of publishing firms that likewise did not exist in 1965 was large enough and powerful enough *and commercially successful enough* to organize itself into a trade association. That association is now a considerable force within American publishing, complete with a trade journal, a paid staff, and a very sophisticated network of distributors.[4] Equally as indicative of success but of even more significance for the purposes of our present discussion is the fact that by late 1993 and early 1994 many New Age spokespersons, publishers, and writers were beginning to describe themselves as being within, and the New Age movement itself as being, a religion.

Beyond the spirituality and Universalism books that the emerging New Age houses themselves produced and continue to produce, however, lies another, and to me deeply fascinating, fact. Religion publishers, denominational publishers, and commercial publishers with religion lines — three very different entities despite their surface similarities — have all begun within the last four or five years to also produce a steady flow of books on both subjects for the first time in the history of American publishing. Universalism now goes under the guise most often with these publishers of ecumenism and world's religions; but by whatever rubric, books like *The Joy of Sects* by Peter Occhiogrosso[5] and/or expensive, heavily illustrated books about the faith systems of the globe, whether by revered authorities like Huston Smith[6] and/or popular publishers like *Reader's Digest*,[7] have racked up impressive figures in commercial retail sales and a sustained retail shelf presence that would have been unthinkable in Rosie and Johnny's day.

Even more diagnostic of the shifting emphases and changing

definitions of our times and of the inevitability of them all has been the scramble within American Judaism, American Christianity, and American Islam to reinculcate spirituality and spirituality principles into the habits and claimed heritage of their devotees. This scramble is obvious within the homilies and public statements of the clergy and the hierarchies of all three religions. It is even more clearly exposed, however, by the sharp increase in the sheer number of spirituality/mysticism/meditation titles coming out of the respective publishing arms of each of these three dominant faith systems.[8] The push to reclaim spirituality for America's religions, to establish beyond all doubt spirituality's historic presence within each, to kick start the practices of spirituality as a part of daily regimen in the lives of the American faithful — these speak more than does anything else to the impact of recent time upon present time.

The whole of all of this shifting and adjusting would have an almost endearing quality to it (or else a ludicrous one, if the observer were so bent) were it not for the deadly seriousness with which the adjustments and accommodations are being made — and were it not for the deadly seriousness, economic as well as private and subjective, of the battle for survival going on within much of institutional religion in this country.[9]

*   *   *   *   *

One of the defenses for the individual believer against spiritual loneliness, especially against the spiritual loneliness that rises up from religious isolation and disenfranchisement, is wonder — just plain, simple, old-fashioned wonder — that excites both the spirit and the mind. Certainly in these years of transition, while religion in American is being reconfigured and denominational loyalties are failing to hold, the need for wonder and its means has burgeoned among America's religiously lonely.

Within Christianity, which is the bulk of this country's religious census, and especially within Roman Catholicism (and indeed almost all liturgical Christianity) there has long been a doctrine or principle called now by the name "sacramentalization."[10] The term refers simply to the presence of the sacred in the ordinary, to the presence of wonder in the quotidian. At its core, sacramentalization is also the polysyllabic but theologically sound recognition of that most central of spirituality's fundamental precepts, namely, that the sacred interpenetrates all spheres of experience and is therefore apperceptible in all. Blessedly for the heart-weary traditionalists among us, sacramentalization is also a clear way out of the trap of equating God with the sacred.

Well argued, sacramentalization can even be — in fact, accurately and correctly is — a clear way of proving that God and the sacred were never really interchangeable in the first place, at least not inside the doors of institutional religion, but only outside of them in the arena of popular misconceptions. As a result of its broad applicability, sacramentalization, of all the segments of spirituality presently being aggressively claimed and reclaimed by institutional religion in this country, is one of the ones — perhaps even the one — of greatest concern. Books about it abound now, especially in the seasonal lists of Roman and liturgical Christian houses, but there is certainly no lack of such material coming out now from indigenous houses in Judaism and Islam as well.[11]

There are other ways — more subtle sometimes, I think, and less self-perceptive — of achieving the separateness of God and the sacred at an emotionally supportable level. Oddly enough, or perhaps fortuitously enough, these ways have become the common path of both New Agers and secularists, the appropriate concern of both the New Age publishing community and the commercial, denominational, and religion publisher's one.

Beliefs and principles that once were moral concerns with spiritual resonances have wriggled free of religion and asserted their sacred necessity as parts of life. They have, in other words, usurped the tying-together utility of religion without taking on, at least for the moment, all its organizational encumbrances and impedimenta. The most obvious example of this shift is the ecology movement, but so too is the gender equality movement and the conservatism movement, to mention but two others.[12] In each case, religion as Johnny and Rosie knew and understood it has become subservient to the newer permutation — and in some areas of the country and/or among some Americans, a victim of it.[13]

Evidence of this separating out and the substituting of tying-together issues for historic religion is nowhere more apparent than in the world of books where volumes that would once have been shelved by a bookseller or a librarian under religion are now indeed shelved as ecology, women's studies, lifestyle issues, and the like.[14] Yet these accommodations seem, in the final analysis, to be only that — accommodations. What is afoot as the twentieth century dies and as the millennium rolls over is far more substantive than mere accommodations. What is happening is reformation — for the second time, reformation. Reformation of and within Christianity, yes, but also reformation of religion.[15]

*　　*　　*　　*　　*

When religion begins to fail a believing community, then that community must come eventually, by way of however much distress and dislocation as may be required of it by the process, to look again at religion with a more analytical — and usually, though paradoxically, much less jaundiced — eye. That is to say that there comes a time or times periodically in all human encounters with religion when the community must begin to separate or to separate once more the substance of faith from the forms of faith.

In order to survive its own contradictions of desire and its own internal conflicts of mind against soul, the believer individually and the body of believers corporately must consider the nature of their discontent and discover its resolution. Invariably the disclosure is of the vitality of faith and the obviatedness of its forms.

This process is cyclical and it certainly is everywhere present in

the history of humankind and religion. The time of its most recent re-occurrence is now; and America too, since about 1992, has
come down more and more emphatically on the side of loyalty to
God, not to form.

The kicking over of institutional, sectarian, and doctrinal traces
together with an accompanying boldness in mixing and matching
from many different religious forms in order to reconfigure a new
(but not yet clear) definition of religion-as-institution are everywhere as evident as they are and were inevitable. Nor is there any
doubt but that the clarity of new definition will in time be exposed.
America is a believing culture and our boomers a believing generation.[16] And while religion may theoretically exist without God,
the business of approaching God is instantaneously, from its first
tentative gesture to its paeans of well-formulated praise, religion.

To believe that there is, or that there may be, or even just that
there might be some Other outside of, but active within, time and
experience is, so far as anyone has ever been able to ascertain,
one of the few absolutely universal possibilities with which every
human intelligence at some point flirts. To believe in that possibility just enough to take even the most hesitant steps toward
considering what it might mean and what actions and reactions
commitment to it might require is religion.

There is no great mystery to such subtle pivoting, of course.
Acknowledging the possibility that Atlantis might have been is
a neutral act of intelligence, for instance, right up to the point
that one begins to envision exactly what such a place would have
been like and what it would have meant to the Europe of pre-
history. At that precise moment, the intellectual acknowledgment
becomes an imaginative occupation. Just so, weaving in, once it
begins; re-image-ing in, once it commences; tying possibility to result; connecting subjective "maybe" to objective "so therefore" —
all of these things become, in the life of the spirit and its concern
with the possible divine, religion. That that religion will grow to
have form as well as substance and that its substance will in time

exceed and shatter its form is no more, apparently, than a fixed principle of human affairs.

God talk, once it begins and without regard to whether or not it is mature enough to discern God as creator of the sacred rather than as coequivalent with it, is religion; and religion must engage the totality of all its believer's/believers' parts if it wishes to remain stable as a religion. When the body and its mind and emotions are suppressed, when their good health and good sense are made hostage to doctrine, or when the soul's rich experience is impoverished by sectarian dogma, then the latters and not the formers must go for the believing spirit's sake. Religion in such circumstances must indeed re-configure.

＊　＊　＊　＊　＊

As surely as the New Age movement was the first herald of a crumbling form in American religion and as surely as New Age spirituality was the demand of the soul for its birthright of extravagant exercise and elegant existence, just so surely have the demands of the mind and emotions already begun to suggest at least some of that coming new form that will become American religion.

While pentecostalism is a distinctly Christian movement, ours is nonetheless a distinctly Christian culture; and the rapid — like fire through droughted forests, in fact — spread of Pentecostalism, sectarian or not, must be treated as an indicator of where religion's new forms are going to be found in the near future. That place is in the ecstatic. That place is in the elevated and celebratory state of awareness in which the self escapes its own confines in worship and joins others like itself in a universal and wordless glory. That place is also, at least in our culture, distinctly African American.

Call it black spirituality, call it "soul," call it neoprimalism, call it whatever you may, the truth is that that totally physical and physically total celebration of God-among-us is in the American experience contained in African American religious practices. African American form likewise is now, and is increasingly going to be, part of both the new wine of American faith and of the new wineskins that will contain it.[17] God, in other words, is from now on to be heard in the thunder as well as in the still small voice of whisper.

Aside from several recent and very fine studies of their emerging importance within America's reforming practice of religion,[18] there is no greater proof than the plethora of books about the whole complex of African American worship.[19] What began as a small stream in late 1993 has swollen into a broad river that continues to flow ever more fulsomely.

In subject matter the books about the African American religious experience run the gamut from academic studies of African American influences on America's new faith practices to very populist and popular rap Scriptures[20] and biblical commentaries by African American preachers to meditation books and confessionals[21] to study guides about it (or, as is the case with most such books, about how to grab and hold on to it).

The books about African American religious practice are everywhere and the demand for them apparently insatiable in this time of our emerging from discontent into action. More subtle, however, and certainly neither ecstatic nor broadly populist are two other cries of the body for a place in the new forms and practices of American religion — the cry of the intelligence to be satisfied and the cry of the mind to be properly defined.

*   *   *   *   *

Strangely complementary to the shift toward ecstasy, both of these new demands or emphases arise out of the physical sciences and our expanding body of knowledge about the mechanical structure of both ourselves and our situation. From the theory of relativity and quantum physics to Stephen Hawking's ruminations on the big bang theory to popular applications like Frank Tipler's *Physics of Immortality: Modern Cosmology, God and the Resurrection of the Dead,*[22] there has been a steady progression of books from *every* segment of American publishing about the ever-diminishing separation zone between physical science and religious belief.

If these books did not, by and large, ever make megaseller-dom, they did and do sell well enough to justify their continued publication, *and they sell among those readers who, by bent of prior training and stature, have probably been those most able to disseminate and popularize their message* of divinity increasingly revealed and of religious mystery increasingly objectified and validated. But because "mind" — or more accurately, too much "headedness" and emphasis on reason — is perceived as the culprit that stole soul from religion and helped thereby to create our present state of religious disease, mind and its findings are going to be of less popular importance to belief and of less interest at least for awhile than are mind and its findings about itself.

Until, in other words, the intellect, the reason, the consciousness — the head part of us by whatever name — can persuade the spirit in us that it has learned its proper place in the greater scheme of things and has gained the requisite humility to remain in it, all the imbalances of the decades immediately preceding 1965 will continue to appertain. And if that statement is not often said aloud yet (and almost never committed to paper, I might add), the fact still remains that nothing is so impacting the reforming of American religion as are the new fields of computer science, artificial intelligence studies, neurobiology, neurochemistry, neuropsychiatry, and so on.

From the early works of Freud and Jung right down to the work of men like Turing and Penrose and Edelman, there is an informing flow of interpreted data that has militated for a repositioning of mind from master to tool and of consciousness from self to its state. These are major shifts and the very stuff religion is made of. They have, however, already gained effective popularizers, perhaps most obviously, as we have already noted earlier, in books like those of Daniel Dennett, *The Mind's I: Fantasies and*

Reflections on Self and Soul (with Douglas Hofstadter) or *Consciousness Explained,* to pick but two.[23] Even a cursory glance at the sales figures for these and similar books confirms their successful penetration of the more general market.

*   *   *   *   *

If we can see ourselves — and now we must — as more than intellect or awareness, and since we experience ourselves as something more than soul, we have come — or appear certainly to be coming again — to mystery. To the inscrutable. To spirit. Spirit, inextricably part and parcel of body and soul and bound to them. Spirit, the complementary third and compelling portion of our self, and the final part of our totality. Spirit.

Even the mind boggles before spirit's greater greatness and toward the hope its presence brings. Yet spirit, while it may indeed know itself (or so the ancients teach us), cannot be known to mind. Spirit elects, in fact, to deny itself to mind as does the cloud deny itself to the sea, though both are water and equally agents of it. Spirit projects itself instead like a cloud darkling upon the surfaces of the sea. And we say, being sea, that we bear the image of the cloud but are not it.

It is mystery; and as mystery, already unabashedly part of the emerging new religious sensibility in America. We touch its possibility and are guaranteed in a way that exceeds even the comfort we gain in exercising soul. God in the thunder, God in the whisper, God in half-caught image.

And we reach back to those who first bore the mark of image — to the saints and holy ones of Judaism, of Christianity, of Islam. We reach back to them, their lives, their words, through books, dozens and dozens of books since 1992 about their lives and their theophanies, their visions and their epiphanies.[24]

But there is more to the business of saints and more to looking back than mere fascination with the words they may have left or the inspiring and sometimes hyperbolized lives they may have lived. There is, especially in Christianity, the image, and it is image more than word that speaks our present language of religious suggestion.

In the visual images, and especially in the icons, of Christianity there is the saint realized. The painting or the illumination affirms the spiritual biography of its subject and burns with glory its viewer, branding the memory with possibility and hope. The icon is even more. The icon is the transparency beyond which the sacred rests eternally on display. To absorb the icon is to permit the self to become the saint and adore the One of whom the saint is nothing more than window and sign.

The image is force released beyond the restrictions of words, and it can, just that easily and readily, become idolatry. It has always been so regarded by Judaism and to some lesser extent by Islam; but the times have slipped, and we with them, into a postmodern, postliterate existence where the luxury and the economy of image can no longer be denied. Whatever Christianity may become in the next millennium, it will without question — it must, in fact — become powerfully visual in its promulgations of itself. And whatever American religion — or American monotheism, for that I think is what really is emerging out of our times — whatever American monotheism may or may not become, it will take from Christianity, if not the practice of the icon, then the devotional and even the didactic use of art.

*   *   *   *   *

I have spoken several times in this chapter already of religion's being currently in a state of reforming in this country, and there is little question that our religion is presently very much a work in progress. Intermediate and modernist forms of religious practice and of doctrine have been shattered; new and very old ones are only just beginning to find renewing shape and juncture.

During the ten or twelve decades that lay between roughly the mid–fifteenth and the mid–sixteenth centuries, the Christian church underwent similar such upheavals of redefinition for reasons remarkably like those that have evoked our current disarray. As we all know, the Christianity that emerged from that time of reassessment — appropriately enough called then and ever since then by the name of the Reformation — was an entirely new and wholly different phenomenon from the western church that had spawned it.

What is happening in our own time is an analogous process.[25] As I have already indicated, what is being reformed will not in my opinion be limited to Christianity this time around but rather is much more likely to be a reforming of religion per se and probably of monotheism per se. I have little or no idea just what the final result of all of this will be in its particulars, but based on precedent I think we can predict at least some of its generalities; because regardless of what may happen doctrinally or liturgically, the new alignments and changes must historically be consonant with religious story, if not with religious practice or particularized dogma.

Humanity's sacred stories are sacred, the faithful would say, because they are true. I certainly am not inclined to challenge that position, but I do want to offer a more pragmatic addendum. Sacred stories are also sacred because they have survived; and central to that process, they have survived by suffering evolution. That is to say that by shedding what was irrelevant and retaining what was sustaining, sacred story arrives, almost by default, at what is valid. Moreover, the sacred story of America's three religions is, right up until the axial age, the same core story. The potential impact of that one fact — that is, the presence within one avidly seeking culture of three distinct world faith systems with a common and storied origin — is incalculable.

In this country at this time, each of our three major faith systems is caught in the same social, cultural, generational, and political foment as are the other two; and each is experiencing similar pressures from similar sources both inside of, and external to, their own religious communities. Given such near identicalness of origins and current circumstance, it is difficult to imagine that any one system will effect the adjustments of its next two or three decades in isolation. Rather, it seems more likely that the reformation of each will take place in terms of the evolution of the other two. It seems just as likely — if not more so — to me that we may even see a reformation of American religion as an integer.

Either way, for all three faith systems (as is true for any religion anywhere at any time), the sacred stories must be examined, recodified and reestablished before any change within the believing community can be effected — and usually, even before any can be meaningfully begun.[26] Thus, the first Reformation was both heralded and sustained by a plethora of new Scripture made available to the laity at large for the first time through the technology of printing and the accessibility of many translations into the vernacular. Everything from the Geneva Bible of our Pilgrim Reformed-faith fathers to the King James Bible we as Americans still love best came to us up out of that era of reforming agitation.

In just the same way there has been a most remarkable — a totally unprecedented, in fact — surge in Bible publishing in this country in the last four or five years. The exponential growth in the number of Bibles sold has been matched as well as fed by the remarkable number of new and/or revised and/or reissued translations, the growth in the number of versions of Holy Writ available, and the expansion of applications and editions. So obvious and so feverish was this activity in 1993 that the year came to be referred to across the publishing industry as "The Year of the Bible."

The other, more dangerous and equally significant thing that apparently happens as religion(s) go(es) into reformation is not just a broadening in the dissemination of sacred texts but also the recodification of them. During the original Reformation, codification was one of, if not the, major issue that led to the convening of the Council of Trent in 1545–47, 1551–52, and again in 1562–63.

In response to the pressures of protesting believers demanding reform of the faith and as a means (near the end of the council's deliberations) of distinguishing orthodox Roman Catholic Christianity from the Protestant and Reformed Christianities that were clearly viable by 1562–63, the council declared a Roman canon of Scripture that was and still is considerably different from that of Rome's rebellious offspring. That same process is now at work again in this country, being especially visible within most branches of Christianity and with respect to such presently noncanonical works as the Gnostic text the Gospel of Thomas.[27]

Where the original Reformation could lay claim to and be stimulated in its searching by the technological advances of printing and written vernaculars, our present reforming has been stimulated and informed, and now to a large extent driven, by the advances of archaeology and scholarship. The discovery of Ugarit in 1928 and its subsequent excavation led to the unearthing of a veritable trove of Canaanite documents dating from the second millennium B.C.E. This sudden windfall of information about the myths, worship customs, pantheons, traditions, and social patterns of those in whose presence Israel lived has had an inestimable impact on Old Testament studies. It has led to the retranslation of many previously questionable passages and to new and very different interpretive commentary on others.

Ugarit was followed, after World War II, in rapid succession by the discoveries in 1945 at Nag Hammadi and in 1947 of the Dead Sea Scrolls at Qum'ran. All of the wealth of variant texts, of manuscripts known up to that point only by references to them in other texts, and of materials previously unknown has completely reshaped exegetical thinking and biblical scholarship. The wealth of new and rediscovered materials has not, however, stayed demurely behind the cloistered gates. Rather, it has burst forth like the opening salvos of a cannonade and entered into the thinking, conversation, and study tools of even the most rural and remote of America's Christian, Jewish, and Islamic communities.

There has never before been such a storming of the canonical doors by laity.[28] One or another of the many popular texts on the Dead Sea Scrolls[29] has been on religion bestseller lists in one journal or another almost continuously since 1993; and in cooperation with the Israeli Antiquities Authority, the Library of Congress in that year bowed to the same kind of demand by placing twelve fragmentary scroll manuscripts on public display and then on a national tour, where the viewing sites were mobbed by the curious.

Much of the excitement, the urgent sense of new information demanding to be evaluated and of recently discovered texts waiting to be incorporated, has been an impetus (as well as the intellectual and scholarly base) for the search for the so-called historical Jesus. As previously unknown and/or unseen and/or variant Christian texts have been discovered and made available, many of the traditional stories of the four established Gospels and much of the Christology derived from the established New Testament Epistles have been brought into question, or at least into thoughtful reconsideration. Out of this reconsidering has risen the uneasy sense that perhaps what twentieth-century Christianity in America has accepted as Savior is not actually the Jesus who really was but the Jesus of some first-century heretical Jews on their way to becoming Christians, all of them with a private agenda of religious justification idiosyncratically their very own. Since contemporary doctrine, praxis, and liturgy are all based on the Jesus of the pre-1945 Gospels and the Christology of the apostolic letters, to bring these primary sources into scrutiny is to bring into question almost the whole of Christianity as such and the absolute entirety of its formalized structure.

The enormous popularity, then, of books like *The Five Gospels*[30] or of other, similar works by popularizing scholars like Dominic Crossan, Marcus Borg, and Raymond E. Brown[31] is neither an idle nor a fanciful vogue. It is, rather, the deadly serious pursuit of deadly serious believers looking to the reformation of the vehicle and expression of their faith. Yet before we as observers of this process look too particularly at the search for authentic beginnings and currently credible texts, we need to acknowledge — to render explicit, that is — something that up to now in this discussion has been more or less implicit, and that is the presence among us of the "American religion."

*   *   *   *   *

American religion, when used as I intend it here, is that construct which supersedes and confines the particular faiths that function within it — which supersedes and confines in much the same way that a lens supersedes and confines the photographer's view of what parts of actuality he or she can by deliberate intention record or even respond to.

How, by such a definition, to distinguish American religion from American culture would no doubt be beyond my skills as well as the limitations of our present purposes here were it not for one simple fact: American religion has — or at least in my opinion has — a sacred text, and that sacred text is, to continue my metaphor, a lens through which the sectarian canons, creeds, and practices of each world-faith body operative in America must be seen and by which they are most surely confined.

I wish neither to be flip here nor to put myself in a position of being seen as such, but any serious discussion of American religion must, in my opinion, consider the thesis that I. Frank Baum is to American religion as Moses is to Judaism, Christianity, and Islam and that the *Wizard of Oz* books are as the Pentateuch.

There is about religion anyway and anywhere an irony, an inherent paradox, an almost delicious schizophrenia: Religion deals with the sacred in terms of the human. It is, in other words, as earthy and messy and communal as spirituality alone is prone to being elegant and ethereal and individual. When religion forgets, as in our earlier years, to incorporate spirituality, it does so to its own detriment and even to its own endangerment. Wisely, therefore, as currently, religion employs spirituality as a tool in its various endeavors, but inevitably in doing so it sullies spirituality, usually distressing the more fastidious among us in the process.

Fastidiousness has not historically been a principal concern of Americans, however, in either our politics or our religion. That is not to say that we celebrate disarray so much as to acknowledge the fact that we distrust orderliness, especially hierarchal orderliness. The divine right of anything above the center, be it king, bishop, or abstract principle, is suspect among us, as well such things should be. We are, after all, the recent descendants, most of us, of an immigrant history and a peasant heritage. The gods and rulers of such a people as we are need — all of them — to be held on a short tether lest they float too far above us.

This part of our national character, if things progress over the next few decades as they have over the past twenty-five, this part of our national character may become our national character, the one immutable in our cultural composition. Whether that actually happens or not, the taste for the egalitarian, an adept's fondness for caricature, and an empathetic belief in particularized and customized principles as prime premises are certainly part of us now. And why not? They are the three commandments of the religion of Oz. And however we may come to shape, or may already be shaping, religion in this country, we can no more escape Frank Baum than we can ignore Moses and still have the faith of our fathers.

For each of America's three dominant religions as for the 97 percent of our citizen-believers, what will be in the coming millennium, while not yet apparent, is nonetheless already present and already textualized. To catch a glimpse of the sacred as it will be addressed in our future is best done, arguably, by looking more closely at a particular religion among us and, logically, by looking in depth at the numerically and culturally dominant one of Christianity. But if our looking is to have any virtue, any diagnostic and prognostic benefit, we must keep ourselves honest. We must not look at Christianity in America, we must look at Christianity in the land of Oz.

— *Interlude* —

An Exemplary Tale

JOHN SHELBY SPONG is a tall, rangy man whose face has the deeply creased, weathered look of a midwestern farmer despite the fact that, at least so far as I know, Jack Spong has never been either a Midwesterner or a farmer. He is, instead, the Right Reverend John Shelby Spong, Episcopal bishop of the Diocese of Newark, and arguably the best-known Anglican living in America today.

Spong's fame — or his notoriety, as he himself would phrase it — stems from a certain painful iconoclasm that he has pursued for the past twenty years to his own anguish and the media's delight. The two are, of course, inextricably connected. Bishop Spong's ability to effectively challenge the tenets and practices of his church has rested in large measure upon his willingness to speak without personal reserve graphically and frequently to the secular press.

Going public has rarely been known to endear anyone to his or her fellows; it has never been known to endear a clergyman to either his peers, his superiors, or the bulk of his co-religionists; it certainly has not endeared Jack Spong. In a very real sense the weathering of the face and the stoop of the frame are, as with our American farmer, testimony to a life that has been spent walking into the wind and against the storm.

Most often cited in the popular press for his ordination, without Church sanction, of homosexuals to the Episcopal priesthood, Spong has consistently made the point that his defiance of the established Church in this matter is, and always has been, one first of abiding pastoral concern for the whole-person needs of homosexual believers and, secondly, one of conviction that the call of God to the priesthood is just that, the call of God. As such, it is no longer subject to either the authority or the questions of the human beings who constitute only the visible part of the institutional body.

Once persuaded of a particular man or woman's holy vocation and of his or her preparation for clerical orders, he says, "I have and I will continue to lay on the hands of apostolic succession, ordaining them to this ministry in the name of the Father, the Son, and the Holy Ghost. Amen."

We were speaking of all these things, Jack Spong and I, during one late afternoon and early evening together at the Top of the Mark in San Francisco in the fall of 1993. Originally our appointment had been arranged by his publisher as an interview session. The two of us, though both Anglican and both passionate about it, had never met before that afternoon. I, of course, knew of his work and he of mine, but that aside, we were strangers to one another.

Our meeting was occasioned by the fact that he had another book, *Resurrection: Myth or Reality?* slated to come out four months later in March. Like all of its predecessors — *Born of a Woman: A Bishop Rethinks the Virgin Birth and the Treatment of Women by A Male-Dominated Church; Living in Sin: A Bishop Rethinks Human Sexuality; This Hebrew Lord: A Bishop's Search for the Authentic Jesus; Rescuing the Bible from Fundamentalism;* and so forth — *Resurrection* was already showing every sign of becoming a bestseller for Spong and for HarperSanFrancisco, his publisher.

Any bestselling author, regardless of the godliness or lack thereof of his cause, is fair game for the press anyway, but a bestselling author in religion is especially fair game for press like me who specialize in that part of American culture. I had, to say the least, jumped at the chance to spend an hour or two with Jack Spong. So we were sitting, he and I, over tea and flat, tasteless crackers in the midafternoon dusk of a late November afternoon high atop San Francisco.

The man before me, the man across the incredibly small and wobbly cocktail table from me, was worn thin. There was no question of that, and he made no pretense to the contrary. He had fought the good fight for twenty years now, the fight against judgmentalism, against spiritual arrogance and doctrinal absolutism, against anti-intellectualism and slavish legalism, against all the sins and failures and pretensions that human institutions are heir to. This newest book was only his most recent attempt to carry the same unbending message of revolution within faith out to the broadest audience possible. If that meant the distraction and the "notoriety" of another popular bestseller, then so be it. Jack Spong's responsibility was and is and evermore shall be to his Lord. Fifteen minutes with the man would convince even the most cynical interviewer of that central and informing fact. This man is a man in service to his God.

He speaks softly, wearily, again almost unguardedly, not only of our shared denomination within American Christianity but of the faith at large. He speaks, sadly, of "the Church Alumni Association" and of his own three daughters who belong to it, "simply because 'Church' is no longer there for them, no longer viable or relevant or any of those buzzwords that mean, basically, connected. 'Church' gets in their way."

As one who also has children in both the boomer and the Xer generations, I can nod my head in the right places and have it be genuine rather than perfunctory. He and I can both bow to the ache he is describing, the grinding, ubiquitous sorrow of the believing parent who has found both solace and form within the institution but who knows right down to the pit of his or her soul the deterrent to faith and practice that the matured child is finding in that same institution.

"Oh, God," he says in the fading light that comes in the windows from across the bay, and there is no hint of the melodramatic. Jack Spong is speaking now to a fellow believer and a fellow Episcopalian, not to the press. Because he can do that and because he can make that separation, we are destined to become friends as well as coconspirators, though neither of us knows that on this singularly damp, singularly blessed afternoon.

San Francisco grows dull outside the windows beyond us, seems briefly to hesitate, then turns on its evening lights and exudes a sigh of enormous relief as its night begins. Bishop Spong speaks on, not so much about books now, for we have long since forgotten what it was we came as professionals to do, but about the work he has done and the work still ahead, about the costs — his own and those of his supportive New Jersey diocese — of fighting to open up the institution and its canons, about ordained gatekeepers and their arrogance, about pastoral love and Christian love, about intellectual currency and its place within the life of faith.

The bishop's charge, it eventually becomes apparent, is not to Anglicanism — or at least not to Anglicanism as he perceives that body — but to Christianity in general, to Christianity in America and Christianity at large in the world. His is a call to inclusiveness, to private obedience, to a strange and media-savvy humility (which is as possible as it is rare), and to an agony of self-immolation on the pyre of belief in a turbulent time.

As San Francisco turns to its evening occupations and as our waiter grows finally impatient with our nonalcoholism to the point of obviously wishing us gone, the bishop asks me to dinner with him and his wife. I accept, selfishly reluctant to have our time together end. He nods as we agree upon where we are to meet for dinner and turns to go for Mrs. Spong. Already half a stride away from me, he turns back and says, as if in explanation of our whole afternoon, "It really gets down to this — all of my life's work gets down to this — to the one central question: How shall we sing the Lord's song in a strange land?" He nods again, and this time he does not turn back.

*   *   *   *   *

By the rivers of Babylon, there we sat down, yea, we wept, when we remembered Zion.

We hanged our harps upon the willows in the midst thereof.

For there they that carried us away captive required of us a song; and they that wasted us required of us mirth, saying, Sing us one of the songs of Zion.

How shall we sing the Lord's song in a strange land?

If I forget thee, O Jerusalem, let my right hand forget her cunning.

If I do not remember thee, let my tongue cleave to the roof of my mouth; if I prefer not Jerusalem above my chief joy.

These are the words of the 137th Psalm, one of the best-loved, most frequently spoken hymns of the Jewish and Christian Scripture.

In 586 B.C.E., King Nebuchadnezzar of Babylon completed the conquest and sacking of Jerusalem, carrying away from that holy city with him the best and finest of Judah's young men and women and, with the exception of the prophet Jeremiah, the godliest of Judah's prophets and priests. Confined in Babylon for the seventy years that were to constitute the Babylonian Captivity, those captive Jews were to learn in exile and adversity the lessons of obedience, humility, and faithfulness. The 137th was born out of that agony of soul and real history, out of that reconversion to constancy within change, to belief beyond expediency.

"How can we sing the Lord's song in a strange land?" The question has haunted the faithful for the millennia since its first asking, just as surely as it will always haunt my memory of one particularly poignant evening in San Francisco. But more than that, "How can we sing the Lord's song in a strange land?" already haunts the coming millennia. It is, in fact, their central question, if one is Christian in America today.

– 9 –

What Christianity Is in the New Age

WESTERN HISTORY has traditionally been segmented by great events of the soul. Like all history, the West's is dotted and punctuated by wars and spiced with the names and accomplishments of formidable leaders; but the eras of our experience — be they labeled as B.C. and A.D. or by the more recent terms B.C.E. and C.E. — are referenced in terms of our communion with one possibility, that of God.

Most of the recorded part of that history has had to do with the notion of an intervening, temporally active, self-sacrificing God — or at least two thousand years of it, by common agreement, has. The persuaded Christian — within whose company I include myself — would argue that all of western history has been so occupied. He or she would argue, in fact, that the progressively self-revealing God of Christian adoration is the God of all history and — an even more assertive principle — that all of history is itself the progress of that self-revealing by the Creator to the creature. Regardless of one's private persuasions, however, and regardless of how one interprets the years from Eden to Calvary or from Eden to Medina, the inter-testament age still stabs through over half the world's experience, pinioning it to a center and transepted pole as securely as any arrow ever pierced its target and then was held true there by its own accuracy.

Such stabbing — such a dramatic assertion by half the world's cultures that religion is the first cause of culture as well as of experience — such everywhere-employed rhetoric, both reveals our absorption with religion as the most utile way to engage the sacred and also, however subliminally, makes of history a religious text. It makes history subject to religion and, subliminal or not, that has been a powerful idea among us for at least two millennia.

Seeing history through the lens of God's self-revealing — and both Judaism and Islam share with Christianity this penchant, albeit to different conclusions — has utility for a community of faith. Reading history as a religious text can likewise be an instructive exercise for individuals within the community. It is an informing perspective that as a Christian I would defend earnestly and with every bit of my apologetic abilities. Like many of my fellow Christians, I by this very means gain much of the theology with which to tend my private decisions, integrate my own faith, and become accepting of my own limitations. When, however, as had happened by 313 c.e. or thereabouts, the political and/or enfranchised majority of half the known world takes on a basically theological perspective and begins to apply it as template to public decisions or to those outside of the community of faith, then something bizarre happens.

To begin a discussion of American Christianity with Constantine's Edict of Toleration in Milan may be a bit extreme, but hyperbole has its place in argument as it does in memory, and certainly nowhere more appropriately so than here. The ever-present danger and ever-possible corruption of seeing history as religious text is that one can all too easily inflate humanity's place in history — can much, much too readily inflate humanity's agency in it, in particular. Thus, the burden of preventing the reenactment of history's anguished sorrows by manipulating history's present actors becomes a holy cause: God's work being done, for God's text is being employed.

If western history is segmented by the events of the soul, then

God knows it is also most tragically and painfully pocked and scarred by the false and/or inappropriate application outside the communities of faith of a precept intended for ritual use inside of them. The holy wars of western time all find either their overt origins or their justifications in just this one spot. And they obviously were able to do so only after the good Emperor Constantine opened the floodgate and recognized, probably unavoidably, the right of Christianity to become without price the claimed faith of all. By that one act, a new kind of majority was created, one constituted by principle and belief rather than as in previous times by locale, tribe, class, race, or economic interests.

Yet to give history and the emperor their due, adjusting the present and the future by adjusting contemporary conduct is neither a politically nor a morally stupid idea. The problem is that as an idea it is just not a theological or devotional one. It is too limited for that, lacking as it does all the salvific possibilities of grace, mercy, mystery, and even divine surprise. What such manipulation attempts, ultimately, is to man-make the sacred, to hammer it out of the stuff of human conduct and then to blast it immutable in the heat of moral determination. What such manipulation lacks, however, is all the requisite parts for the goal it proposes. It would enact upon the physical in the name of the spiritual without any of the soul's wisdom and with none of its consolations.

American Christianity, of course, and as many, many of us know all too painfully well, has come to just such a place. "Déjà vu all over again" as more of us than just Yogi Berra have begun to say.

*   *   *   *   *

American Christianity. There is no such thing, of course. That is, the phrase "American Christianity" implies an integer, and there is no integer. Instead, as we have already said, there are by the most recent accounting over twenty-five hundred distinct presentations of American Christianity. Patently, anything so diverse in presence is neither an integer nor even a fit subject for many generalizations or informing analyses. Divisiveness itself is the analysis. Saying that, however, does not release us from some need to look, if not at American Christianity, then at a noncohesive, noncohering mix of presentations of Christianity as they are currently extant in North America, especially if we truly hope to discover and explore the nature of the sacred in our lives today.

Based strictly on their loose theological affinities, there are presently five main divisions of Christianity in this country.[1] In descending order of their respective censuses, they are: Roman Catholic Christianity, Evangelical Protestant Christianity, Mainline Protestant and Liturgical Christianity, Pentecostalism, and Other. Such a list is obviously meaningless, however, without some commentary.

For example, the most rapidly growing segment in the list is also the next to the last one. Pentecostalism, as we have already observed, is rushing into America's religious sensibilities as fire rushes into dry brush...and for the same reason. Pentecostalism is the aggressive, ecstatic, humble, broken, unpretentious, celebratory, loud, rejoicing, triumphant, multiracial, purely spiritual assertion of God as Holy Spirit active upon the physical persons and cognitive souls of his beloveds, his believing and adoring children. Pentecostalism's dignity is its lack thereof. Its strength is a strength to be coveted by all of American Christianity, for Pentecostalism is the one part of that body that presently rests where vital religion always must rest — in paradox.

Pentecostalism is, and is growing, because it treats of the soul, the body, and the spirit. Its vulnerability is, of course, that it lacks history to stabilize itself and a tradition of the elders to describe itself. Its hubris is that it can or may or will emphasize one of the believer's three parts — in this case, the soul — and its experiences over those of his or her other two constituent members. And Christianity — American or otherwise, divided and severed or whole and integrated — is the religion of the body, soul, and spirit. The presence in equal measure of all three and the eternal presence and integration of all three are two of the no more than five or six litmus tests against which any faith scheme claiming Christian affiliation must be tested and proved compliant. Failure to acknowledge all three parts of the creature and of the Creator is to participate in something certainly, but in something that is quite definitely other than Christianity. The equality and eternity of body, soul, and spirit is, in short, an absolute against which many a pretender has already crashed.

Second, in our listing of Christianity's five large divisions in America, the presence of "Other" as a category is basically offensive, both to me personally and to the millions of believers who fall into that grouping. In fact, were the various denominations that constitute "Other" to be grouped together on any basis except their very divergence from each other and from traditional Christian theology, those millions of Americans in "Other" would be American Christianity's largest single body. Instead, "Other's" men and women belong to separated but recognized bodies like Christian Science, Jehovah's Witnesses, Mormonism, and Scientology that are huge in numbers and in financial empowerment but that are positioned in supra- or extracanonical theology and works like the Book of Mormon or the writing of Mary Baker Eddy and L. Ron Hubbard.[2]

The defining sectarian titles of my five categories must also be remarked upon as well. Had I been asked to draw up a list of the divisions of American Christianity twenty-five years ago, it too would probably have shown five sections, but those five would have been defined differently. Most noticeably, Mainline Protestantism and Liturgical Christianity would have been two separate categories instead of being two halves of one.

The death of Mainline Protestantism and of Liturgical Christianity has been so much and so loudly touted as a fact of late that I almost doubt their demise. In fact, every time I hit upon another jeremiad about the dying mainline, I am reminded of a late uncle of mine who for fifty years practiced general medicine in the most rural parts of pre–World War II western Tennessee. As the only physician within literally hundreds of miles and in the days before emergency rooms and triage nurses, Uncle Kay was forced to devise his own system for deciding whom and what to treat first in any general emergency. He evolved a system based on what he called "the holler factor: Anything making a whole lot of noise is never as bad off as it thinks it is." (There was a corollary: "It's the quiet ones that need you.")

Certainly we all are more comfortable speaking of the diminishment, rather than the demise, of something so historically vigorous and influential as Mainline Protestantism and Liturgical Christianity have been, so I am particularly grateful to have the crutch of avuncular wisdom to lean on here. But whether the issue be dying or simply regrouping, the truth is that I, like many other Americans, am diminished by the decreasing role of Mainline Protestant and Liturgical Christianity in America's national life. Columnist Ken Woodward spoke for many of us when he wrote recently in *Newsweek* that the Mainline Protestant denominations — the Presbyterian Church (USA); the United Methodist Church; the Evangelical Lutheran Church in America; the Episcopal Church; the American Baptist Church; the United Church of Christ; the Christian Church (Disciples of Christ) — "for more than a century helped define America and its values," and their loss will be the country's as well.[3]

A second difference between the definitions on my list of categories and those that would have appeared on a similar list twenty-five years ago is the fact that Pentecostalism (under the denominational names of Assemblies of God, Church of God, International Church of the Foursquare Gospel, Church of God in Christ, and so on) would have been included in, rather than segregated from, Evangelicalism (many Baptist bodies including the Baptist General Convention, Church of the Nazarene, Churches of Christ, Reformed Church in America, Salvation Army, and so forth) and maybe even from Charismatic and Fundamentalist groups which, as you will note, do not even appear as a separate entity on my list anymore.

The reason for this shift is, certainly, in no small part due to the bursting forth of Pentecostalism and to its growing segregation of itself — its almost aggressive distancing of itself — from Evangelical and Charismatic Christianity.[4] But it is due far more significantly to the growing emphasis by Evangelical Christianity upon the political and the moral — upon the new holy wars.

* * * * *

That girding up for battle, that sense of divine commission to effect the national life theologically, is Evangelicalism in these last years of the twentieth century in America. It is not Christianity; it is Evangelical Christianity. And that is a massive and distinguishing difference. Although not all Evangelicals adhere to their division's dominant and most publicly visible stance of enforced moral reform through political activitism, such a stance is nonetheless presently the centering and cohesive one in their part of American Christianity.

Curiously enough — or perhaps ironically enough — many, many Roman Catholics who would never for a second consider abandoning either their liturgy or their doctrinal heritage and worldview, find themselves deeply drawn to the theocratic message of Protestant Evangelicalism. So strong is that attraction that it has led to serious and authoritative reassessments recently of the real doctrinal issues that hinder full cooperation — almost full cohabitation — between the two bodies.

The most powerful of these recent reassessments is the document *Evangelicals and Catholics Together: The Christian Mission in the Third Millennium,* issued in May 1994. A position paper resulting from intense conversation convened in September 1993 and sustained by fifteen leaders (such men as Chuck Colson, Fr. Avery Dulles, S.J., Fr. Richard John Neuhaus, Dr. John White of the National Association of Evangelicals, and the life), *Evangelicals and Catholics Together* bears the endorsement as well of twenty-five other leaders — leaders like Pat Robertson and John Cardinal O'Connor, not to mention equally well-known but less spectacular pairings like Os Guinness, Bishop William Frey, and Professor Peter Kreeft of Boston College.

The document, which runs to eight full printed pages, opens by declaring: "We are aware that our experience reflects the distinctive circumstances and opportunities of Evangelicals and Catholics living together in North America.... We together, Evangelicals and Catholics, confess our sins against the unity that Christ intends for all his disciples.... The two communities in world Christianity that are most evangelically assertive and most rapidly growing are Evangelicals and Catholics.... As Evangelicals and Catholics, we dare not by needless and loveless conflict between ourselves give aid and comfort to the enemies of the cause of Christ," and so on. It concludes with the words: "Nearly two thousand years after it began, and nearly five hundred years after the divisions of the Reformation era, the Christian mission to the world is vibrantly alive and assertive. We do not know, we cannot know, what the Lord of history has in store for the Third Millennium.... We do know that this is a time of opportunity — and if of opportunity, then of responsibility — for Evangelicals and Catholics to be Christians together."

There are a number of other logical and easy reasons beyond those of theocratic and millennial concerns that may also encourage Evangelicalism and Roman Catholicism to want to meld over the coming few years. At 58 million strong and growing, Roman Catholic Christianity is the largest single body of faith in this country today. That alone is a compelling enticement to conversation, especially to a kindred group that, like Evangelical Christianity, has slipping numbers domestically but not globally. Moreover, Roman Catholicism, like Evangelicalism, believes in the power of the printed word. It has the second most active Christian denominational publishing program in the country — second only, that is, to Evangelicalism's in terms of intention toward, and impact upon, the general culture.

Furthermore, as the sale of Roman Catholic publications and, even more emphatically, as the sales and popularity of books by Roman Catholic authors like Fr. Joseph Girzone and Fr. Andrew Greeley have grown, they have borne home the point to everyone that Americans yearn — nostalgically yearn — for that religious heritage of which the symbols, trappings, and liturgy of Roman Catholic Christianity are the central representations in the popular imagination, if not in its daily reality.

And nothing could have more vividly reenforced and underlined our awareness of such broad yearning toward the enthroned and the elevated than did the discovery that Roman Catholicism has one other thing that much of American Christianity, and especially Evangelical Christianity, lacks — a hero. Even fairly agnostic Americans have embraced "the Mighty Pole," and so great was the public fervor when His Holiness came to Denver in 1994 that one national telecaster was heard to blurt out over the airways, "America is receiving her pope!"[5]

Thus, Roman Catholic Christianity is in the enviable position of finding its message of symbolic heritage, well-ordered regimen, elegance, and conservatory practice welcome among many Christians and its leader lionized by even more. Union from and with such strengths could dramatically change the face of American Christianity within the next half decade, should it occur.[6]

Nor do I mean to imply that such greater communion would be to the greater advantage of either party. It would, quite clearly, be of greatest benefit to the thus-engendered whole and of equal cost and reward to the participants. Despite presently slipping numbers at home, in other words, Evangelical Christianity is growing abroad; and it is certainly the dominant segment of American Christianity today in terms of visibility and urgency. And with or without new alliances, Evangelicals may indeed manage to reverse their slippage over the next few years and/or reconstitute themselves as America's numerically largest group of Christians by other means. There is some reason, in fact, for thinking that such a thing is more than possible.

Within Evangelicalism, it is common parlance to speak both of "the subculture" and "the core group." These phrases are descriptive of the approximately 11 million Americans who presently actively follow the tenets and faith patterns of Evangelicalism (i.e., belief in the infallibility of Scripture, the virgin birth of Christ, the resurrection of all peoples, the triune nature of God, the indwelling of the Holy Spirit, and so on). The phrases are also a recognition of an undesirable line of separation between Protestant Evangelicals and the other 78 to 80 million active Christians in this country.

The line is undesirable in part simply because lines are, especially lines among those sharing a common religious heritage. From an Evangelical point of view, the line is even more undesirable, however, because it is an honest acknowledgment of a present reality, namely, that Evangelicalism's most natural allies lie within the next echelon of 78 million–plus Americans who are active, churchgoing, but not Evangelical, Christians.

These millions are natural converts; they are also natural bridges into the culture at large. To reach and persuade them has become a primary purpose of Evangelicalism. For that reason, Evangelical Protestant Christianity has become over the past few years more and more attentive to publishing its message by whatever means possible — by books and television, radio and magazines, CD-ROM, and Internet.

So successful has this effort toward outreach been in laying claim to the larger title of "Christian" without a qualifier that most unaffiliated Americans now use the terms interchangeably or, even more frequently nowadays, never even use the qualifying "Evangelical and/or Protestant" adjectives at all. Christian Books, Christian radio, Christian magazines, Christian music—all are no longer "Evangelical and/or Protestant Christian" but simply regarded as products of the whole, a potent perception from which to build membership and public stature for the subgroup.

Evangelicalism's success has also had a self-fulfilling and self-enhancing property in other ways as well. As Evangelical publishing in all its forms has penetrated and persuaded the larger Christian and even non-Christian culture of its moral and value-oriented positions, it has managed to become itself more successful in the process. The result has been an Evangelical publishing industry, especially in books, magazines, and videos, that looks out just as assuredly and confidently as it looks in.

The resounding commercial success of political books coming from Evangelical houses was the first indicator of just how desperately America at large wanted such a message. That success has now led to the next publishing thrust, that of the value-oriented story. Political treatises persuade by argument. Stories — especially mystery stories, historical fiction, and romances — persuade by example and pleasure. And once more, as we noted earlier, the astuteness of Evangelical Christianity's efforts is being confirmed by sales figures and by the product performance of a line of books. Faith fiction, inspirational fiction, Christian fiction — call it what you may, the now burgeoning flow of books that tell their plots without profanity, sexual impurity, or physical violence and with virtue-rewarding, happiness-affirming result has hit a responsive chord in America's cultural nostalgia, if not in its religious memory.[7]

All of this shuffling and reshuffling — this do-si-do-ing in a typically American square dance of faith — has led some observers to postulate a cataloguing of American Christianity that by 2000 C.E. would read as: Evangelical/Roman Catholic Christianity, Pentecostal Christianity, and other. The problem with such a suggested change, even when it is as here offered with tongue in cheek, is that it is still very premature; and while joking about contradictory and delicious possibilities — especially about holy ones —

is pleasurable, it also can dull one's acumen with the rasp of its own perversity. So we must, bearing the ever-possible future in mind, nonetheless keep our fancies rooted in current actuality; and the operative truth presently is that the number of traditionally Protestant American Christians claiming Evangelicalism is dropping precipitously and that there is indeed every reason to assume that Roman Catholic Evangelicals will remain just that — Roman Catholic Christians with Evangelical characteristics and sympathies but with thoroughly Roman loyalties.

What does seem already to be happening right now, however, and what does give credibility to the notion of an imminent recataloguing, is twofold and of real consequence to any predictive understanding of American Christianity. The first is the breakdown of hierarchal organization and/or the decentralizing of every part of institutional Christianity;[8] and the second is the separation out of christianized value systems from the context of Christian worship and the body of Christian worshippers.

If within the next five to ten years institutional, centralized, or denominationally administered Christianity does indeed crumble (and I for one believe that it will),[9] and if our social concerns can in fact be more totally politicized, then much of the present confusion about, and tension between, religious unity and theocratic mission will be resolved, at least for awhile. Moreover, should such a shaking out and a realigning indeed be under way, history itself suggests that they will be followed by a shedding of what has not worked and an emergence of what has.

That is, history — anybody's history — would suggest that somewhere in the five present divisions of late-twentieth-century America's several Christianities and in the interacting tension, differences, and alliances among them there is indeed some much smaller, much humbler center around which the most theologically graceful elements of each are already coalescing. Whatever that attracting center is, once completed it will in time, I believe, become the Christianity of post-Christian America — or as schol-

ars and commentators are now saying, of the post-Christian era —
for once again western history is being segmented by events of
the soul.

*   *   *   *   *

Ozian theology — that is, the basic religious sentiment informing post-Christian America — is that of an accessible, vulnera-
ble, and fundamentally good-hearted, omnipotent monocot in a
color-coded universe whose evils are personifications that can be
surmounted and whose principles can be circumvented by noble
intention. It is not an uncomfortable theology on an average day,
or even an inutile one on a bad day. It is certainly an acquies-
cent — sometimes even a cordial — backdrop for the interplay of
nostalgia, healthy balance, imaginative symbols, practical morality, social stability, easy ethics, and basic human respect. What
it is not is Christian. And what it lacks — what is remarkably
lacking in generic American monotheism as well as within the
present emphases of the three largest segments of Christianity[10] —
is much real attention to the passion of the soul, to the life of
the hungering spirit, to the variousness of the immutable sacred.
Oddly enough, sadly enough, almost inevitably enough, these
have slipped through the fingers of both institutional America and
most of institutional American Christianity. They have, as we have
seen, become instead the purview of the last two categories of
Christianity — namely, Pentecostals and Other — and of loosely
affiliated seekers.[11]

Yet there has come another crier in the land, an insistent and
persistent rallyer of both the faithful and the susceptible, one who
will, I suspect, not be denied. To take any sighting on American Christianity now without looking at it through the scope of
millennium is like trying to make tomorrow's rocket fuel out of
yesterday's gun powder.

Millennium. Suddenly it is everywhere. Millennium, with its

suggestions of end time, its near-proofs of the long-suspected life beyond life, its scent of prophetic mystery fulfilled. Millennium, with its galvanizing excitement of a better possible or just a less boring actual. Millennium, with its awe-ful stirrings of repentance and its self-flagellation, with its readout of disease and flood and famine, of violence in our streets and in our bedrooms, of wars and rumors of wars as the stuff at last of Armageddon, Rapture, and Ragnarok. Millennium.

None of us can say the word without at least a small catch of the breath. What if? Just what if...?

Wherever pervasive excitement, however subtle and however discounted by the urbane, wherever endemic excitement goes with its promise of change and interruption, we become — all of us, willy-nilly — like children following the scent of secrets in November conversations. And when, as with millennial conversations, the possibility is of more than interruption in an ongoing regimen; when rather it is the pledge of some completion, some realization beyond mere interruption, some transforming redefinition of life as we living have known it; then the religious heart lifts up with glory.

It may also sink, of course, as do some experienced hearts before any party, with fear and trembling; but it knows itself at last as religious. It knows once more the emotions of the spirit as well as those of the soul and the body. And it is those spiritual emotions that, in my opinion, are the American Christianity that is to be the Lord's song in Bishop Spong's strange land.[12]

The Lord's song will always in America be sung by an American choir. No one, least of all me, would want to change that ever-changing, ever-reconfiguring, ever multicultural and multiracial lifting up of many voices, nor even to vary by one whit the suggestions, forever folded into its choruses, of spacious skies and fruited plains for pilgrims' feet. Those too are appointed parts of the sacred. But what has been lost to us as Rosie and Johnny's struggling offspring is something that has never really been part yet of Christianity here in North America at all, some things whose roles, right up until Rosie and Johnny's time, were played at least in part by those very plains and skies and sainted, or merely self-appointed, feet.

The new Christianity, for instance, whether it ever becomes institutionalized again or simply remains parochial and confederated, will speak the words of difference between goodness and righteousness in a way that the spirit has always known and that frontier necessity could not afford to differentiate. The religious spirit, especially the religious spirit at large in Ozian goodness, yearns toward the more that is a humble and sweet and sometimes playful righteousness, that is goodness vivified by holiness. It yearns and it will find. (It must find, if for no other reason than that it otherwise will stultify in the overmuch kindness of end-time morality.)

The heart of the religious in all times and cultures cries out, "By what right can I praise you and by what Name do I call you?" for like the lover with the beloved, the religious heart cannot sustain the agony even of holy passion without some release of its expression. But when Yahweh, one-time god of thunder and latter-time God of the cathedral, becomes present and perceivable God of both, awe slips in with a steely glory, and praise becomes a redemptive energy in human affairs.

To the extent that end times are endings and to the extent that the Christian imagination in post-Christian America can come to occupy that promised vision, then to just that extent will the American practice of Christian love also be redeemed. Without the anxiety of a tomorrow or the unknown burdens and constrictions of a next week, the self, like the small child of holy parable, spends itself in affection and never knows to call its givings by such intentional names as self-sacrifice or concern, learned respect or religious obligation. That release alone becomes the body of hope made tangible and the substance of forgiveness made actual.

And, if not last, then certainly among the most immediately

obvious, whatever else a reforming American Christianity may already be divesting itself of as rapidly as possible, it is divesting itself most rapidly of the intellectual mannerisms of the Enlightenment, mannerisms and conventions that disparaged a meditative passion and the antique metaphors of holy love, that excoriated conclusion by faith and impugned premises based on received truth. At the same time, we who are Christianity in late-twentieth-century America seem to be stripping from our theologies as well those countering conventions that drew in the sands of God the lines of literalism and called them orthodoxy or that by using dogma to dress the mind have girdled as well the naturally evolving wonder of a progressive revelation.

So the times shift as only twice before they for the Christian have shifted — once at akedah when Abram lifted a knife over Isaac's chest in agonized willingness and once on Calvary when the god of thunder let that knife fall in an agonized willingness of his own. Between the two were two millennia, and between us and the latter another two. We wait. Being Christian in America, we wait, most of us knowing that we may also live to see.

– 10 –

A Confession of Faith

THIS BOOK HAS, from its inception as an idea in its publisher's head, rested on the premise that one of the most defensible and informative ways of determining the actual place, definition, and role of the sacred in contemporary America is by tracking the commitment of dollars and time adult Americans make to (and to which parts of) what for lack of better terms we call the sacred/spiritual/religious in life. To objectify the subjective through the most private and intimate of its observable expressions, in other words, or to use books as an index by which to articulate at least the larger patterns of the American soul.

I believed from the beginning that such was a sound thesis. I still believe it to be. I thought in the beginning, and still think, that it is hardly a humble one; and I never thought it was a fully realizable one. Yet for all its inherent limitations and for all the time-dated fragility of its conclusions, a study of where the sacred/spiritual/religious sensibilities of most of us and/or of large subsets of us are is of use.

Obviously to the cadres of professional religionists — media, religion writers and editors, clergy, seminarians, denominational administrators, and the like — any template that is both diagnostic and predictive of the subjective life is of considerable worth. Likewise one can assume that the book community — librarians, chain buyers, publishers, even independent retailers and ordinary readers — has a vested interest in seeing itself and its market from every possible vantage point and especially from the vantage point of an area of major industry growth like sacred/spiritual/ religious books.

While I hope I have with integrity addressed those obvious interest groups, and while I am enormously grateful to them for their role as justification for this project, I must confess that my abiding and sustaining motivation has been individual...not personal, but individual.

I am Christian. I often say to audiences of mixed religious persuasions as a kind of caveat against a too-ready acceptance of any interpretations or conclusions I may be about to publicly make, that I am "dangerously Christian." That does not so much mean that I feel some kind of need to convert the rest of humanity to my own way of being, but it does mean that I address the world as one who holds the sacred as expressive of God; as one who believes in the tripartite personness of God and of all human beings, and in the equality and eternity of all those parts; as one who understands time-history as theater of representation for reality not presently graspable beyond some stage directions and an assigned place in the cast; as one who knows redemption from meaninglessness and relief from debts owed and never repaid as having been provided for by the deliberate self-spending of God himself; and as one who presumes to know personally and be known by that God.

With very few variations or expansions, those beliefs are the core of Christianity, the four or five litmus tests I mentioned earlier as being the ones against which any pretenders must be tried. How they are applied to everyday life, of course, is the very stuff of denominational, sectarian, and individual differences.

For instance, in saying that I am one who presumes to know personally and be known by God, I mean not just the obvious exercises of prayer and meditation that inform any religion, much spirituality, and even a good deal of just plain reverence for the sacred. No, I mean instead that as a Liturgical Christian, I presume to know and be known in so personal a way as to consume the sacrificial body of God and drink of his Blood in order not only that I may remember that unimaginable sacrifice and bear its evidence in my body but also that I may be in God and God in me.

As a religious exercise, it is called theophagia, and it is not a particularly attractive one to sell in its candid explication. It is, in fact, downright unattractive. It is also very primitive and not much different in external appearances from the practices of many early and/or aboriginal peoples who likewise must eat their god. There are differences that make that particular analogy a paper tiger for me, but this is not the place to argue theology.

The point, instead, is to say that one of the principal characteristics of Christianity is that it is not a very beautiful religion. The point is, as Moses noted so long ago, that the Christian God isn't very Ozian. He's a hard sell, mediawise. The point also is that life in a culture that lives Oz and claims Christian can be a very numbing experience. Confusion becomes a religious contagion that weakens the most private chapels of the soul and debilitates the spirit.

If as an individual, however, I can hold a contour map in my hand while I look across my near and not-so-near landscape, I will conceptualize my own bit of land more realistically and more efficaciously. I will increase my intimacy with it and thereby my sense of my own relationship to it. I will certainly know the better whether to treasure or despise it. So this has been an individual as well as a professional project, one for just plain individual individuals among whom we all are. But leaving the matter there is abandoning the simile before it is complete.

To stand with contour map in hand like some surveying landlord or ambitious tenant working to better understand is not to understand; for we are the land, and the borders we describe and the contours we discover are our edges of possibility and the sustaining nexi for our watering and our drainage. And more perhaps than anything else, that description is my religion.

I am the eternal land I look on and can never be and into which, like the seed in fall, I shall drop in order that I may be, yet not I as was the seed but I as was its God-drenched mystery.

Lord Jesus Christ, Son of God, have mercy on me, a sinner.
Lord Jesus Christ, Son of God, have mercy on me, a sinner.
Lord Jesus Christ, Son of God, have mercy on me, a sinner.

Notes

Chapter 2

1. A third entree to the sacred — philosophy — needs some mention here as well. Certainly just as time-honored as religion and far more so than many forms of contemporary spirituality, philosophy is not the tool of the lay or untrained seeker. For that reason it has not been part of the current American mix which, at its heart, is a populist and generalized one. The exception or qualification to this is "Eastern Philosophy," a term that is clearly growing in popularity and utility. More than to philosophy per se, however, the term in common parlance refers to nontheistic religions originating in Asian rather than European cultures. In general and for clarity as well as economy, I have chosen here to use the more sectarian but much more specific terms *Buddhism, Zen,* the *Tao, Confucianism,* and so forth instead of *Eastern philosophy* whenever possible, treating those worldviews as what they are — nontheistic religions that borrow heavily from both spirituality and theistic religion to compose a third but related means of engaging the sacred.

2. The need for making a distinction between religion and spirituality is a product of our current state of striving toward the sacred. So too is our ability to regard spirituality and religion as equivalent means for conceptualizing and entertaining the sacred. While the latter is theological and organized, the former may or may not be either; and each adapts some characteristics of the other to its own purposes. Even in the popular mind, however, they are becoming increasingly distinct approaches. Perhaps one of the best summaries of this part of contemporary American sacred phenomenology can be found in a section of the Roof Report titled "The 'Religious' and the 'Spiritual,'" in *A Generation of Seekers,* ed. Wade Clark Roof (San Francisco: HarperSanFrancisco, 1993), pp. 76–79.

3. Readers interested in greater detail about the many laudable demographic studies conducted in this country over the last decade will

want, because of the sheer volume of possibilities available, to check not only periodical literature but also the complete listings of recent work by such demographers as George Gallup, Fr. Andrew Greeley, and George Barna.

4. The incongruity here, if there be one, is that poetry is primarily (and regrettably) a book-tied art form while religion is hardly restricted to books. The corrective principle, however, is that books report, reflect, and integrate into religion what is happening, even among those for whom personal reading is not popularly assumed to be a routine or high priority. Witness in this regard excellent recent studies like Harvey Cox, *Fire From Heaven: Pentecostalism, Spirituality, and the Reshaping of Religion in the Twenty-first Century* (New York: Addison-Wesley, 1994).

The second corrective principle is that popular misconceptions often prevent a clear-eyed look at the facts, especially in religion; and the facts are that there is no large segment of organized religion in this country that can legitimately be said to ignore at least sectarian books. Consider in this regard, for example, books by Benny Hinn — *Good Morning, Holy Spirit* (Nashville: Thomas Nelson, 1992); *The Anointing* and *Lord, I Need a Miracle* (Nashville: Thomas Nelson, 1993); and so forth. The number of Hinn copies in print that are of a Pentecostal nature is well into the millions now.

As a further addendum we might also note that there is a fourth — and so far as I know, rarely if ever mentioned — index of contemporary American involvement with the religious, spiritual, and sacral: the sales performance and analysis-by-types of the music industry, where the available data seem to be consistent with those of the book industry. Within popular Christian music, for example, where a significant proportion of retail sales occur in Christian Booksellers Association (CBA) stores and where albums, tapes, and disks are therefore tracked under the same system as, and almost as if they in fact were, books, the data are already available for making such an assumption. We know from CBA statistics, for instance, that the popular Christian music industry topped $500 million in sales in 1993 and that 38 percent of Christian music consumers have begun buying that material only within the last five years.

5. The mapping of trends in the book industry is done primarily by *Publishers Weekly*, a trade journal that for over a century has reported on book, and especially on English-language book, publishing

and retailing in this country and abroad. My position as religion editor for that magazine has undoubtedly prejudiced (though, I trust, not invalidated) my belief that book traffic and the patterns of book sales furnish the most trustworthy guides to the actualities of subjective activity. Whatever else it may also have done, my post certainly has been an exhilarating as well as a singular vantage point from which to watch the evolving, current situation.

6. The fact that this book focuses on the American scene should not be interpreted as meaning that only America is undergoing a spiritual, religious, and philosophical upheaval. That is simply not the case. The National Opinion Research Center at the University of Chicago, one of the world's most respected producers of demographic studies of the sacred, released in mid-1993 a new study, Fr. Andrew Greeley, "Religion Not Dying Out around the World," in *Origins,* June 10, 1993, concluding that worldwide belief in God is greater than ever before. Readers who want to investigate this issue in (literally) graphic detail will find Joanne O'Brien and Martin Palmer, *The State of Religion Atlas* (New York: Touchstone/Simon and Schuster, 1994), an excellent place to begin.

At the same time, however, we must remember that our contemporary experience of subjective reconfiguring is far more intense in America than elsewhere at the moment. The *Wall Street Journal,* in an editorial dated April 4, 1994, made this point quite succinctly. "The United States," the paper wrote, "remains one of the most religious nations on earth and by far the most religious country in the Western world."

7. Of the total retail book sales in this country, wholesalers represent 30 percent of volume. Of that segment, Ingram's share of market is greater than 50 percent.

8. Sandee Brawarsky, "Getting Religion: The Market for Books Exploring a Variety of Faiths Continues to Grow," *American Bookseller,* June 1992, pp. 22–28.

9. It is important that the distinction being made here is quite clear. Inspirational titles have in the past achieved bestsellerdom on a sustained and recurrent basis. See, for example, the remarkable performance of books like Norman Vincent Peale's *Power of Positive Thinking,* Anne Morrow Lindbergh's *Gift from the Sea,* or Catherine Marshall's *Man Called Peter* during the mid-1950s. The pertinent difference here is that between types of material, that is, between the purely inspirational as opposed to the instructional, investigative, and informa-

tive that inspires, as in, for example, the books of M. Scott Peck. There are also some bestsellers — those of Robert Fulghum come most immediately to mind — that sit more or less upon the cusp of this difference, with one foot dangling into each side.

10. For more expanded views on both these points, see my comments in *MultiCultural Review,* June 1994, p. 63, and John Wheeler's essay "Themes for the 90's: A Rebirth of Faith," *New York Times,* December 29, 1990.

11. Barbara DeConcini, letter to the editor, *New York Times Book Review,* May 22, 1994.

12. The phrase "generation of seekers" has also spun off other similar ones. When, for example, *U.S. News and World Report* did a cover story on "Spiritual America: In God We Trust" for its April 4, 1994, issue, the masthead photo of an American mass was captioned "A Nation of Seekers: America seems a more spiritual nation today than it was at its founding." It is worth noting also that from mid-1993 through mid-1994, *Time, Newsweek,* and *U.S. News* alone produced over a dozen such cover stories on spirituality and religion in America, a degree of popular national coverage that would have been inconceivable a decade ago.

13. This set of defining birth boundaries is the one employed by Roof, *A Generation of Seekers* (see n. 2). There can be some slight, if insignificant, variation among demographers, however, most commonly in extending the baby boomer birth years to 1969.

Boomers, in addition to everything else, are also the most studied generation ever to occupy a place in American history. There are, in fact, so many treatments of them and of the sixties that shaped them that I am reluctant to cite particular ones. Two of the better known, however, are probably Paul C. Light, *Baby-Boomers* (New York: W. W. Norton, 1988), and Todd Gitlin, *The Sixties: Years of Hope, Years of Rage* (New York: Bantam, 1987).

There are also several other demographers who, like Roof and Fr. Andrew Greeley, specialize in the study of religion/spirituality/sacredness patterns and who investigate all Americans, not just the boomers, from that point of reference. Among these, one of the most frequently cited is George Barna, whose generational demarcations differ slightly from those of Roof et al. Barna, who likes to continue the *B* artifice, refers to the generations born between 1963–69 and 1977–84 by the label of the "busters" and those between 1984–89 and the present by the label of the "baby bulgers."

Barna, by the way, breaks his own pattern by labeling Rosie and Johnny's generation of adults born before 1926 as "seniors." My own generation of Americans born between 1927 and 1945, however, he labels as "builders," not an unpleasant banner under which to run. Interested readers may wish to consult any of the annual Barna Reports (Ventura, CA: Regal Books, 1991–) for additional information about all five of these generational groups.

14. That distrust, as we know, has also produced a countering reaction among many Americans, most commonly in (or as) Evangelical and/or Fundamentalist and/or Charismatic Christianity or, though in vastly smaller proportions, in the Nation of Islam.

15. Readers wanting a more complete view of this unique period and, more important, of contemporary interpretations of it, should also review Robert Ellwood, *The Sixties' Spiritual Awakening* (New Brunswick, NJ: Rutgers University Press, 1994), or the current works of ordained religionists like Fr. Andrew Greeley and Tex Sample.

From a sectarian view, few commentators could be more hospitable than Os Guinness. His *Dust of Death: The Sixties Counterculture and How It Changed America Forever* was first written in 1971 and has recently been updated (Wheaton, IL: Crossway, 1994) to keep abreast of our evolving understanding of what the sixties did indeed do to American spirituality, religion, and sense of the sacred. Frankly Evangelical Christian, Guinness has an easy candor about his own stance that enhances, rather than diminishes, his analyses and conclusions.

There is, of course, also no lack of recent, more popular/populist titles within this field of sixties diagnosing by writers with more various, and usually conservative, credentials behind their postures. Books by Cal Thomas, William J. Bennett, Rush Limbaugh, and the like come immediately to mind as falling broadly but definitively within this category.

16. I am provoked to use this "weekend" metaphor by two close friends, Marilou Awiakta and Joe Bruchac, both of whom are Native American authors with considerable followings and impressive sales figures to their respective credit (most recently, *Selu: Seeking the Corn Mother's Wisdom* for Awiakta and *Dawnland* for Bruchac, both from Fulcrum Press of Golden, Colorado, in 1994.) As writers within the field of Native American spirituality, both are approached continuously, or

so they rather dolefully claim, by well-intentioned people who begin by saying something like "I have these two free weekends coming up this fall. Where can I go to learn Native American spirituality during one of them?" As Awiakta always concludes, "Need I say more?"

17. In this regard, see particularly *Madame Blavatsky's Baboon* by Peter Washington (New York: Schocken Books, 1995).

Chapter 3

1. The term "generation" can imply a cohesiveness and a cultural cause-effect relationship that do not entirely appertain, at least not in so diverse a society as ours. They certainly will not appertain in the remainder of this discussion, where hereafter I will be using the word more as a convenience than as a sociological tool. (It should also be noted that Roof, *A Generation of Seekers* [see chap. 2, n. 2], frequently offers this same caveat and that in my earlier references to his work I have tried always to use the term in a manner consistent with his own employment of it and with his conclusions.)

2. As reported in *U.S. News and World Report,* April 4, 1994, pp. 48–59.

3. "Why We Pray," *Life,* March 1994, pp. 54–63. See also "Talking to God," *Newsweek,* January 6, 1992, pp. 39–44.

4. Cox, *Fire from Heaven* (see chap. 2, n. 4), is a bit more daring and simply calls this phenomenon "primalism." When I first began to employ the term "neoprimalism," his work had not yet been published. I would argue also that there is a kind of acquired or "neo-" quality anytime such a set of practices and perceptions occurs within a technologically advanced context.

5. Though we tend to think in terms of bookstores when we think about new books and where they are moving, it is important to remember that libraries are the source of choice for many readers. So sensitive are librarians to the current increase in demand for religion/sacred/spiritual material that they have begun an active campaign to participate in trade shows and exhibitions where such materials are announced and to incorporate training sessions in both their state and national professional meetings on how to access such materials more efficiently. *Library Journal,* the professional journal of the library trade, expanded its pro-

gram in March and again in November 1994 to include greater ongoing coverage of religion, primarily of Evangelical Christian, books.

6. This could almost be said of people who read any kind of books. Betty Eadie, *Embraced by the Light* (Placerville, CA: Gold Leaf Press, 1992), commanded a place on both general interest and religion/spirituality bestseller lists for months and also commanded one of the biggest advances ($6 million from Bantam by early June 1993) ever paid for a book's paperback reprint rights. Of course, *Embraced* was followed onto the charts by others within the genre, like Dannion Brinkley, *Saved by the Light* (New York: Villard, 1994), written with Paul Perry, or RaNelle Wallace, *The Burning Within* (Placerville, CA: Gold Leaf Press, 1994), written with Curtis Taylor.

7. The strength of prophecy books was brought home to me rather graphically one afternoon when I was talking to Dr. Henry Carrigan, a member of the adult reference staff for the Westerville (Ohio) Public Library System and religion columnist for *Library Journal,* about a new book on Nostradamus that he was reviewing in galley and by which I had not been favorably impressed. "Good or bad," he said, "it's Nostradamus, and we simply cannot keep him on the shelves. As soon as a new book comes out, the calls start coming in, and as soon as new copies of old titles come in, they're circulating as fast as we can accession them."

8. Titles with impressive sales figures in this particular subcategory tend to be cult or underground bestsellers rather than general trade ones. There are exceptions to the cult/underground principle, of course, Shirley Maclaine, *Out on a Limb* (New York: Bantam, 1983), being an example of a very early one. *Out* was also the first book to make it socially acceptable to talk publicly about being engaged by the Other, undoubtedly due in no small part to Maclaine's celebrity as an actress. Presumably, as New Age becomes more and more mainstream, more and more of this kind of material will find its audience through mainstream outlets without the need for a personality author.

9. Barbara Marciniack, *Bringers of the Dawn: Teachings from the Pleiadians* (Santa Fe, NM: Bear & Co., 1993), is exemplary of the cumulative, underground performance of this kind of title. Since it was first published in September 1993, *Bringers* is now in its eleventh printing and sales in almost every month since have exceeded those of the preceding month. A sequel by the same author, *Earth: Pleiadian Key to*

the Living Library, was published in November 1994 by Bear, and its sales to date have exhibited equal strength.

10. The credibility of the researchers being attracted to such study has also increased rather steadily. See, for instance, Harvard psychiatrist John Mack's work on alien experiences as catalogued in *Abduction* (New York: Scribner's, 1994).

11. One of the most poignant letters I ever received from a bookseller I received in July 1994 from Bess Garrett of St. Bede's Books in Baltimore. "This summer hardly a day has gone by here at the store," she wrote, "that I haven't had occasion to think about 'ancient wisdom' in its many varieties, and I'm working hard to expand our collection." What she was expressing was the bookseller's view of what happens when a groundswell begins.

12. A kind of ultimate proof of the populist intensity of this search came in that bastion of secular bonhomie, *G.Q.* There (June 1994) author Russell Shorto overviewed for five full pages (pp. 116–23) the phenomenon, its origins, and its impact.

13. Robert W. Funk, Roy W. Hoover and the Jesus Seminar, *The Five Gospels* (New York: Macmillan, 1993).

14. The "Semitization of Christianity" is the most adequate description I have ever heard for what is happening. Much as I like to coin a good turn of phrase, however, and much as I would like to claim this one, I have to confess that it originated with Rich Scheinin, religion and ethics writer for the *San Jose Mercury News*. Rich granted me free use of the term, "but only with proper citation" (he was only one quarter serious) and only if I didn't scoop him before he could publish his own articles on the subject (they have now run).

15. O'Brien and Palmer, *The State of Religion Atlas* (see chap. 2, n. 6), have documented the presence of over twenty-five hundred such distinct Christian sects and denominations presently here.

16. About ten days after the Catechism's release, I was in the Tattered Cover Bookstore in Denver, one of the country's largest, talking with their religion/sacred/inspirational buyer, Joel Fotinos. Looking over at a ravaged island display of Catechisms, he shook his head. "Most amazing thing we've seen in a long time," he said. "We restock and rebuild that thing about every hour and a half, and then just sit back and watch it melt away."

17. In an article showcasing the house (*Crisis*, April 1994, pp. 40–41), David A. Bovenizen speaks to this point: "Sophia's success — sales of its

every title mount monthly — offers a compelling evidence of the depth of spiritual hunger among Catholics daily, here and abroad."

18. The professional organization for this group is the Evangelical Christian Publishers Association (ECPA), which celebrated its twentieth anniversary during 1994. One of the more interesting trends afoot at the moment, however, is the shrinkage of Evangelicalism in this country, or at least of the numbers of Americans willing to lay claim to that name and/or to the theological and doctrinal tenets by which it has traditionally defined itself.

The 1994 Barna Report (see chap. 2, n. 13), titled *Virtual America,* reports that only 7 percent of American adults now hold such beliefs. That is a slippage of 2 percent over 1993 and of 5 percent over the 1992 Barna Research Group studies which found 12 percent of us claiming Evangelicalism. Whether or not the decline in numbers is a reaction to the increasingly distasteful, popular perception of Evangelicalism as synonymous with the religious Right has yet to be determined, but it does seem to be a possible explanation.

19. See, for examples of this, the recent catalogs of such houses as Jason Aronson, Jewish Lights, or KTAV. Jewish Lights, established in July 1990, is in and of itself proof of the expansion in this field.

20. See chap. 6, n. 2, below.

21. Arnold Kotler, head of Parallax, laughs about the simpler days of 1987 when Parallax was founded. "Back then," he says, "we sent out five advance review copies, all five of them to alternative and Buddhist journals. Now we send out five hundred, most of them to major media who have asked for them."

22. O'Brien and Palmer *The State of Religion Atlas* (see chap. 2, n. 6), estimate (map 6) that there are over 150 Buddhist centers in the United States, but explain (pp. 101–2) that it is "virtually impossible" to know the exact number of practitioners in this country. Most American Buddhists do not belong to organized centers, and Buddhist sanghas here are informal, unrecorded, and fluid. In addition, as O'Brien and Palmer point out, many westerners assume parts of Buddhism, appropriating each into their core faith. Such believers may refer to themselves alternately as Buddhist or as whatever their dominant faith is, as the occasion suits them.

23. There are in fact some observers who, off the record, are now suggesting that the Semitization of Christianity is in part a response to this same principle. That is, by trying to place Jesus of Nazareth back

into a Near Eastern context, we may simply be trying to satisfy a contemporary American need to tap into the spiritual and sacred heritage of eastern religious thought and fuse it into western values like a personal God and individual significance. Whichever way the truth of that one may ultimately be shown to lie, there is a kind of jesuitical zestiness in the introduction of such cultural diversity in our subjective processing of experience.

24. A splendid and wonderfully readable study of the integration of all of these elements into one contemporary complex may be found in Ernest Kurtz and Katherine Ketcham, *The Spirituality of Imperfection* (New York: Bantam, 1993).

25. See Amy Boaz Nugent, "Books to Keep the Faith," *Library Journal,* May 1, 1994, p. 42. Says Nugent: "A quick survey of publishers' religion/spirituality offerings shows that the religious inclinations of today's readers are geared toward the personal."

26. I don't want to belabor this point. Clearly there is a prior history here filled with authors like C. S. Lewis, Charles Williams, Dorothy Sayer, George MacDonald, Grace Livingston Hill, and the like; but as a competitive part of the book-retailing market, the phenomenon is a much more recent one. Compare, for example, the sales of James Redfield, *The Celestine Prophecy* (Cayucos, CA: Satori, 1993), or of Marlo Morgan, *Mutant Message Down Under* (New York: HarperCollins, 1994), against these earlier giants and the distinction becomes immediately discernible.

27. Fr. Andrew Greeley, "Why Do Catholics Stay in the Church? Because of the Stories," *New York Times Magazine,* July 10, 1994, pp. 38–41.

28. As reported in an Associated Press wire-service interview with George W. Cornell, July 2, 1994.

Chapter 4

1. The baby busters, born in the years between the midsixties and the late seventies to early eighties, are not yet a fully formed or formidable force in this country and are therefore not included within the intended parameters of the present discussion. They, however, cannot be ignored either. They are all either knocking at the doors of adulthood or

are already firmly inside it, and their influence upon the subjective values of this country will become formative within the very near future.

Variously referred to as the lost generation, the 13th Gen or, most frequently following Coupland's (*Generation X* [New York: St. Martin's, 1993]) terminology, generation X, or Xers, the busters are approaching 40 million in number and are, as George Barna points out frequently, the first technoliterate generation of Americans. Their impact on our concern with sacred matters, while it has yet to be defined completely, is already being suggested by the increase of titles and sales for relational and family-issues books like aging, caretaking, sexuality, and the like and in books that circumvent dogma, mostly particularly those that circumvent the sectarian. For more on these projections, see Andres Tapia, "Reaching the First Post-Christian Generation," *Christianity Today,* September 12, 1994, pp. 18–23; Shannon Maughan and Jon Bing, "Tuning in to Twentysomething," *Publishers Weekly,* August 29, 1994, pp. 48–52; and Nugent, "Books to Keep the Faith" (see chap. 3 no. 24), pp. 42–46.

Again, for the busters as for the boomers, there is evidence other than books of an ongoing concern with the sacred. Some of the best of these are anecdotal. One of my current favorites involves *Eye On Faith,* the ABC Satellite Radio Network's award-winning Sunday morning talk show about religion. The show's producers were surprised to discover in the fall of 1994 that *Eye* was being aired twice each Sunday by the campus station at Clemson University. According to the station, Clemson students complained that if they overslept, they missed the show, while others — more energetic — protested that a later airing would mean they might be out and about when *Eye* came on. The result: two airings. The producer's reaction to the news: "We were shocked! They're so young, and we had always assumed our audience was older."

Chapter 5

1. In our time of greater access to private information, we are much more aware than former generations were of just how tenuous is any conclusion or argument built up in phrases like "most of us." We are perhaps even more aware of how insensitive, unkind, and limiting such summations can be to particular individuals or groups of individuals. There is certainly no intention here to either mislead or diminish. Unfor-

tunately, however, while "average," "normative," "the majority," and all their kith and kin may not actually exist outside theoretical discussions of human behavior, the truth is that neither can such theoretical discussions exist productively without such summations.

Chapter 6

1. Religions, as well as philosophies, have historically allowed for this premise as well, meaning that it is not nearly so heretical as it may at first blush seem. The presentation most familiar to the average American Christian, for instance, is the "doctrine of progressive revelation" or some variant thereof. While hardly co-creative in our contemporary sense, the tenet does admit of maturation in the creature's ability to grasp the nature of the divine; that is, the ability of the creature to work reverentially within the limitations of a specific era and space without fear of redactionary judgment. Moreover, liturgical Christians receive the same tenet in their established prayers. Consider for example the following collect appointed for the thirteenth week after Pentecost in Saint John's Breviary: "Almighty and Everlasting God, grant unto us an increase of faith, hope and charity; *and that we may obtain what Thou dost promise, make us love that which Thou dost command.* Amen" (italics mine).

2. For an overview of the scope and strength of these phenomena, the reader may want to see my "In Pursuit of the Intimate Native American Spirit," *Publishers Weekly,* December 13, 1994, pp. 29–31, and F. Lynne Bachleda, "Paying Attention to Buddhism," *PW,* August 15, 1994, pp. 38–41.

3. Harvey Cox makes this point brilliantly in *Fire from Heaven* (see chap. 2, n. 4), just as he also argues cogently that this singularly American mix of Pentecostalism, which has spread from us out to essentially embrace the world, may be one of America's greatest contributions to third-millennium global culture.

Although Charismatic Christians are loath to be confused with Pentecostal Christians and vice versa, the two groups do share many characteristics, a similarity that allows them and their praxes to be treated as analogous, if not identical. Readers who are interested in the phenomenon of American Pentecostal and Charismatic Christianity in export will want to read in this regard Karla Poewe (ed.), *Charismatic*

Christianity as a Global Culture (Columbia, SC: University of South Carolina Press, 1994).

4. It is here, in this one place more than in any other, that the enabling role of books cannot be overstated. As a relatively inexpensive, presumably authoritative, very private, and impunious source of information, books have allowed us to explore widely, and without any commitment before the fact, almost every known means of conceptualizing the sacred and arriving at it. They also, being without gatekeepers and ordained interpreters, allow for — even encourage and invite — private, idiosyncratic assemblages.

Even a casual glance at recent bestseller lists in religion reflects this truly impressive and historically unprecedented catholicity of interest. In August 1994 my own magazine, *Publishers Weekly*, which as the trade journal of the book industry is the authoritative source of such data, showed in its hardcover bestsellers two angel books and one near-death one; the new catechism of the Roman Catholic Church and Karen Armstrong's *History of God* still commanding impressive sales; two titles out of the Gnostic/historical Jesus field; two books on spirituality — one general and one Christian; and one pastoral book of consolation.

During the same month the paperback bestseller lists showed three angel books and the Catechism, but added a Zen book as well as keeping one general spirituality title. The only other change was that the paperback list, as one would expect, included two classics, C. S. Lewis's *Screwtape Letters* and Fr. Joseph Girzone's *Joshua,* along with that perennial of comfort, Barbara Jackson's *Stick a Geranium in Your Hat and Be Happy.*

There is, in the consistent presence of pastoral books and books of comfort on such lists — and they are *always* there of late years — confirmation of one other side of our salad-bar ways. I began several years ago to refer to books as "portable pastors," which is exactly what such books as these have become. They have allowed Americans to receive the benefits of clergy with few if any of its hassles.

As any deliberate and concerned clergyman or -woman will immediately point out, this kind of freewheeling, serve-yourself use of clerical dicta is dangerous for both the reader and the writer. It begs for the cult of personality to supersede the humility and restrictions of ordained servitude. It also offers no consumer protection against destructive and/or inappropriate counsel. However unfortunate both those possible consequences may be for individual seekers and their would-be guides, the point still remains that as seekers we are more and more, in all strata of our society, turning to books to find sacred information and consolation; and second, that those of us who are ambitious or called or driven to guide are more and more turning to books as our method of choice for the exercise of that vocation.

5. For a more detailed overview of this phenomenon, see Bob Summer, "The Need to Understand Islam" *Publishers Weekly,* May 9, 1994, pp. 31–32, and, by the same author, "Sufism, Mystical Child of Islam," *PW,* January 9, 1995, pp. 33–35.

Chapter 7

1. The concept of "unknowing" entered the vocabulary of spirituality through *The Cloud of Unknowing,* the work of an unknown fourteenth-century British mystic, and should be seen as what it is: a reduction of the inarticulatable to a manageable point of reference as defined specifically in his/her life and writing.

2. Buddhism clearly differs here and is the most visible and numerically the largest body in America so to do. Though Buddhists are few in number, the influence of Buddhism and Buddhist teachers is growing exponentially in this country and must be taken into account here and in passing. The Buddhist concept of the human being, for example, while it is also tripartite, is a trinity of body, speech, and mind — a significantly different conceptualizing indeed.

3. Thomas Moore, *Care of the Soul* (New York: HarperCollins, 1992), p. xi. Moore's two subsequent books, *Soul Mates* (1993) and *Meditations* (1994), are also from HarperCollins.

4. The most spectacular recent evidence of this surfaced in November 1993, when thirty-two denominations and representatives from twenty-seven countries gathered in Minnesota for a conference titled "Re-Imagining: A Global Theological Conference by Women for Women and Men." Both the liturgy and the intent were such (one prayer reads, "Our maker Sophia, we are women in your image...Sophia, Creator God, let your milk and honey flow..." etc.) that several supporting denominations, especially Reformed ones, suffered defection, schism, and near dissolution as a result, all of this while the secular media had a field day.

5. The "travelogue" metaphor, as we have already noted several

times before, is a particularly powerful and appealing one presently. There is no more exemplary proof of that fact, especially in the general area of spirituality, than the remarkable sales of various editions of the Tibetan Book of the Dead, the quintessential travel book. *The Tibetan Book of Living and Dying* by Sogyal Rinpoche and Patrick Gaffney (San Francisco: HarperCollins, 1992), for example, has been off and on the bestseller lists since its publication, and it still continues to follow that pattern. Bantam Books' 1994 *Tibetan Book of the Dead* by Robert Thurman has also enjoyed brisk sales. Thurman, in his notes and commentary, takes a completely travel-oriented approach, even referring to Tibetan holy men and women as "psychonauts," and the like.

6. Foster's great classic is *Celebration of Discipline* (San Francisco: HarperSanFrancisco, 1983), but it has been followed by a near dozen volumes of elaboration and/or continuation, all from HarperSanFrancisco.

7. *A Course in Miracles* (Glen Ellen, CA: Foundation for Inner Peace, 1975).

8. Marianne Williamson, *A Return to Love* (New York: HarperCollins, 1992), is only one of her several works in this field, all from HarperCollins.

9. Just a few days before I began writing this chapter, I was encouraged and confirmed in it by a phone call. An editor at Religious News Service called to check on some new and forthcoming gardening books, saying that RNS was putting together a wire-service story on the recent growth in the number of books that approach gardening as a sacramental act "because of its invocational qualities."

10. The spirituality writer Angeles Arrien (*The Four-fold Way: Walking the Path of the Warrior, Teacher, Healer, Visionary* [San Francisco: HarperSanFrancisco, 1993] and other books) emphasizes in her work the central position that the aesthetic can play in spirituality. She frequently introduces her point with a short story:

> When you go to a shaman because you are sick in your self, the shaman asks you four things:
>
> When in your life did you stop singing?
>
> When in your life did you stop dancing?
>
> When in your life did you stop being enchanted by stories and particularly by your own life's story?

When in your life did you start being uncomfortable in that sweet territory of silence?

To discover the answers to all four questions, Arrien says — and quite rightly — is to discover the place in time where the illness of soul began and to mark the place where healing must begin. There are multitudinous other spirituality adepts who teach the same principle, of course, but none who do so more succinctly.

11. This translation is that of Robert Bly, who uses it constantly to make this exact point and to whose good nature I am indebted for my own constant use as well.

Chapter 8

1. A charming as well as instructive discussion of this little bit of etymology (which, by the way, has a remarkably long history as a subject of conjecture) may be found in Mariasusai Dhavamony, "Religion," in *Dictionary of Fundamental Theology,* ed. Rene Latourelle and Rino Fisichella (New York: Crossroad Publishing, 1994), p. 819.

2. While several surveys could be cited here to document both our consuming interest as a culture in religion and the almost exclusively theistic nature of religion in America, the most amiable summary of both points probably can be found in the script of NBC's *Today* show for December 10, 1993. Opening with the statement taken from Seymour Lachman and Barry Kosmin, *One Nation under God: Religion in Contemporary American Society* (New York: Crown, 1993), that "92.5% of Americans identify with a religion," show hostess Katie Couric went on to interview Lachman and Kosmin about the data they discovered in the course of their work. Among a whole bouquet of insightful and germane observations elicited in that interview, some seem to be of special interest here. "Being religious is part of being American," Lachman said. "Religion plays as important a role as race, ethnicity, class, or generation" in this culture. He then went on to offer an explanation. "After all," he said, the bulk of our forefathers "came to America looking for the New Zion, the New Jerusalem," in the first place. As a result, "America's religious distinctiveness is unique" in the world and "especially among its democracies." Thus, "Catholicism, Pentecostalism, et cetera in America are not the mirror image of Catholicism, Pentecostalism, et cetera in Europe or Asia."

Sometimes, moreover, the real significance of the American penchant for theistic religion is brought graphically into perspective by the simplest and most obvious juxtapositions. Such an instructive alignment occurred in a July 1994 report in *The Tampa Tribune*. Michelle Bearden, the *Tribune*'s religion editor, in summarizing the data of several recent polls, noted that in 1992 Americans contributed a "whopping" $56.7 billion to religion, a sum that was almost fourteen times greater than the $4 billion we spent on our three biggest sports — Major League baseball, football, and basketball. She also reported that during the same year a cumulative 5.6 billion of us attended church or temple services, compared to the 103 million of us who attended events of those same three sports.

3. "Religiosity" is often a pejorative, though such is not my intention in using it here. As a term indicating a heightened degree of piety or a devoutness and moralism not present in the culture at large, the religiosity of which I am speaking here found for a number of years, especially in the seventies and eighties, one of its more overt expressions in the dramatic growth of Evangelical Christianity. The Barna Report for 1994–95, *Virtual America* (see chap. 3, n. 17), however, reports a shrinkage of that community for the third year in a row.

4. NAPRA, the New Alternatives for Publishing, Retailing and Advertising, of which Marilyn McGuire is executive director, is headquartered in Eastsound, Washington. *NAPRA Trade Journal* is published out of the national headquarters; Matthew Gilbert is managing editor.

5. Peter Occhiogrosso, *The Joy of Sects: A Spirited Guide to the World's Religious Traditions* (New York: Doubleday, 1994). Note as well that Occhiogrosso's is one of the first major studies to treat the New Age as a religion. The author chooses, in fact, to regard it as one of the seven major faiths or sects in the world today and grants it a coverage equal in length to that given to Christianity.

6. See, for example, Huston Smith, *The Illustrated World's Religions: A Guide to Our Wisdom Traditions* (San Francisco: HarperSanFrancisco, 1994)

7. See, as an example, Peter B. Clarke (consulting ed.), *The World's Religion: Understanding the Living Faiths* (Pleasantville, NY: Reader's Digest, 1994). Another rubric that also appertains in this regard is "mythology," especially of Joseph Campbell–like materials. See such lavish and very successful books as *World Mythology*, published in 1993 by Henry Holt with Roy Willis as general editor and with an en-

grossing foreword by Robert Walter, director of the Joseph Campbell Foundation.

8. A *Newsweek* cover story, "Talking to God" (January 6, 1992), concludes that "for bookpublishers, the intense interest in prayer has been a godsend. Astonishingly, the current edition of Books In Print lists nearly 2,000 titles on prayer, meditation and techniques for spiritual growth — more than three times the number devoted to sexual intimacy and how to achieve it."

9. An Associated Press story by David Briggs on January 8, 1994, reported an 86 percent increase from 1988 to 1990 in the number of Americans switching from claiming a denominational affiliation to those claiming "no religious affiliation" in response to survey forms.

In addition, according to Kenneth B. Bedell (ed.), *The Yearbook of American and Canadian Churches, 1994* (Nashville: Abingdon Press, 1994), in constant dollars the per-member contributions to benevolences by American church members dropped by $1.45 from 1968 to 1991. Compounding the impact of this drop is another and ironic fact: Within the same time frame, overall giving by church members rose $56.31 in constant dollars, *but the entire increase was allocated and stipulated by the contributing members to "Congregational Finances," meaning to lo-cal rather than national and/or denominational programs.* The report concludes: "In a society going through major cultural shifts . . . the level of support the church receives from its adherents is a telling indicator of how large a role the church will have in helping define the values in an emerging new order" (p. 12).

10. Fr. Andrew Greeley, arguably America's most beloved and best-selling Roman Catholic writer and spokesperson, published in the *New York Times Magazine* of July 10, 1994, an excerpt from a forthcoming book. Titled "Because of the Stories," the excerpt proposes that Roman Catholics remain in that faith for life primarily "because of the stories" it tells them and the truths it conveys by means of story as opposed to overt didacticism. In the course of making that argument, Father Gree-ley writes: "Catholicism has great stories because at the center of its heritage is 'sacramentalism,' the conviction that God discloses Himself in the objects and events and persons of ordinary life" (p. 40). Few, as always, have ever said it better.

11. Readers desiring to see examples of this phenomenon may wish to look over the current catalogues of such publishing houses as Kazi Pub-

lications in Chicago, Jewish Lights Publishing in Woodstock, Vermont, or Paulist Press in Mahwah, New Jersey.

12. An equally graphic demonstration is a casual glance at the magazine racks in a good, general interest newsstand or bookstore. The proliferation of ecology periodicals is matched only by that of conservative ones. Magazines, especially the upper-end ones, can be almost as prognostic as books, in fact, of what adults are interested in enough to spend significant amounts of time and money on.

13. I think it is fair to say, as do many observers, that religion in America today, especially Evangelical Protestant and Evangelical Roman Catholic Christianity, is to some extent being held hostage to both political correctness and a reactionary fear of spirituality. See, with regard to the latter, an editorial, "Blinded by the 'Lite,'" *Christianity Today,* September 12, 1994, p. 14, and, in the same issue, James R. Edwards, "Testing the Spiritualities," p. 25.

14. One of the consequences of this diffusion or spinning off is that it makes accurate tracking of religion books very difficult. Thus, Cahners Publishing Company reported in September 1994 (*Publishers Weekly,* September 19, 1994, p. 8) that in the period 1991–94, Religion constituted the second largest segment of America's book sales, exceeded only by Juvenile. The "peak month" for category growth, however, was February 1993, this despite the fact that the number and sales of books on or about sacred/spiritual/religious concerns are increasing each year. As I and our writers talk to booksellers and publishers, we are discovering that the inconsistency is semantic. "We don't put that in religion anymore" is becoming a classic retailer response.

The *anymore* is the one word in that phrase that is most indicative of what's actually happening. The book business has a trade term, "crossover," that for years has been used to describe books that could live in both secular and sacred space, books like C. S. Lewis's *Mere Christianity; The Lion, the Witch, and the Wardrobe; The Screwtape Letters;* and the like; Fr. Joseph Girzone's *Joshua* books; Anne Morrow Lindbergh's *Gift from the Sea;* and so forth. What the merchant is reflecting when he or she says "not in Religion anymore" is a kind of ultimate crossover in which, if the present trend continues, every book that does not deal specifically with the intellectual study of religion as a humanistic discipline will have "crossed over" into some other part of the retailer's shop to find shelf space under some other kind of signage. Such diffusion into the more generalized areas of human interest and daily living is, in one single example, a very clear expression of the changes currently taking place in our American culture.

Pat Peterson, head buyer for Barbara's Books, a fairly large chain of bookstores based in Chicago, gave a rather classic example of the whole process in late 1994 when she commented to one of *PW*'s writers that Barbara's, "like any other good bookstore these days, has an exploding Spiritual Growth section in addition to Religion." The reason, according to Peterson, is that "fewer people are affiliated with formal religion, so they don't have a place to turn to for help, and they go to the bookstore." Peterson then went on to say that within spiritual growth as a section, there was yet another burgeoning subsection: "People are looking for books on how to deal emotionally and spiritually with catastrophic diseases." And thus the process of proliferation goes — as well as gives every evidence of continuing to go.

15. Ken Woodward, one of the country's most astute religion watchers, seemed to assume almost the same position (as well as to share some of my waffling about exactly how broad the sweep of this reforming may turn out to be) when he wrote: "There's a new Reformation in American Religion, and this time it is not the Church of Rome but Lutheran and other mainline Protestant denominations that are under siege" ("Dead End for the Mainline?" *Newsweek,* August 9, 1993, p. 46).

16. Roof, *A Generation of Seekers* (see chap. 2, n. 2), for instance, notes that "the children of the 60's know that religion for all its institutional limitations, holds a vision of life," a vision he suggests that boomers are unlikely to abandon, however much they may work to modify some of its configurations.

17. Sparkling evidence of this may be found in the agonized vote in national assembly in Memphis, Tennessee, on October 18, 1994, by the delegates of the twenty-one denominations that constituted the all-white Pentecostal Fellowship of North America to disestablish PFNA in order to make possible one day later on October 19 the establishment of a new organization, Pentecostal/Charismatic Churches of North America, that incorporates all races at all levels of Pentecostalism, from the local congregation to the seminary. Following that historic vote, the Rev. Jack Hayford, one of the movement's most prominent pastors, was quoted as saying that "we have been slow to learn how much the community of faith is shaped by culture" or such a vote would have come much sooner (*The Commercial Appeal,* October 19, 1994 p. B8).

18. In addition to those like Cox, *Fire from Heaven* (see chap. 2, n. 4), see also, for related data, Randall Balmer, *Mine Eyes Have Seen the Glory: A Journey into the Evangelical Subculture of America* (New York: Oxford University Press, 1994). The book is a companion to the PBS series by the same title and speaks very pictorially and poignantly about the interface between Pentecostalism and Evangelicalism.

19. See, in this regard, Rich Sheinin, "The Re-forming 'Soul': The African-American Influence on Today's Religion Books," *Publishers Weekly*, February 13, 1995, p. 43–44.

20. There can be no better example of this than P. K. McCary *The Black Bible Chronicles* (New York: African American Press, 1993). McCary's *Book One — Genesis to the Promised Land* (1993) stayed on religion and regional bestseller lists around the country for several months and was followed in 1994 by *Rappin' with Jesus: The Good News According to the Four Brothers*. The success of both books was said to be about equally divided between African American and non–African American readership.

There is an additional matter to be cited here, and that is that part of the American absorption with and yearning toward the perceived greater spiritual candor and vitality of the African experience is not limited to African American sources. The most poignant and moving example of this within recent memory may well have been the "launch" party for Archbishop Tutu's *Rainbow People of God* when it did indeed publish on October 9, 1994. Even allowing for the fact that Tutu is a popular and heroic figure politically as well as religiously for many Americans, the fact still is that there was standing room only and, by police estimates, over five thousand people packed into the nave of the Cathedral of St. John the Divine in New York City that Sunday afternoon. Charlayne Hunter-Gault, narrator for the event, in her convening remarks called the gathering "the largest publishing party in history."

21. There are far too many examples for me to be very comfortable with citing any in particular. It would be equally wrong, however, to ignore bestsellers like Eric V. Copage, *Black Pearls* (New York: Morrow/Quill, 1993), that stayed on the lists for months or powerful volumes like Lonzie Symonette, *He Calls Me by the Thunder* (Nashville: Thomas Nelson, 1993), or Andrew Young's spiritual memoir *A Way out of No Way*, also from Nelson in 1993.

22. Frank Tipler, *The Physics of Immortality: Modern Cosmology, God, and the Resurrection of the Dead* (New York: Doubleday, 1994).

Some greater realization of Tipler's success in penetrating the popular mind with his message was brought home to all of us when *Omni* magazine chose as the cover story for its sixteenth anniversary issue (October 1994) "Science and Religion: UFOs and God." As its interview subject for that anniversary issue, *Omni* chose Frank Tipler (pp. 89–107; Interviewed by Anthony Liversidge).

23. Daniel Dennett, with Douglas Hofstadter, *The Mind's I: Fantasies and Reflections on Self and Soul* (New York: Basic Books, 1981), is a fine example of what is meant by general market penetration. In its first four months in print *The Mind's I* went through three printings and then was sold to Bantam for paperback publication (where it has gone through several printings and continues in print to the present.) It likewise was a selection by Book-of-the-Month Club, Science Club, Macmillan Book Clubs, and Readers' Subscription. It was serialized as well in March 1982 in *Book Digest*. His *Consciousness Explained* (New York: Little, Brown, 1992) has done as well, if not better, in penetrating through to a lay audience. (For an interesting, more recent example, see Robert Wright, *The Moral Animal: The New Science of Evolutionary Psychology* [New York: Pantheon Books, 1994]).

24. Julian of Norwich has had a particularly evident surge of popularity, as has Saint Teresa of Avila and Saint Augustine. There has likewise been a surprising surge in the quantity, popularity, and breadth of sources and catalogues about the saints and/or of books gathering together in one place the lives and exemplary words of a dozen or so compatible ones. The greatest change in such books, however, has been their inclusion — costly inclusion — of richly illustrated, carefully reproduced examples of sacred art representing the saints. And the greatest growth within the subgenre of "saint" publishing itself has been in books that are in reality collections of sacred art, books that emphasize the representations of the saints more than the saints themselves, in other words. At the same time there has also been a small but noticeable increase from Islamic houses and/or Islamic publishing programs of handsome collections of ancient, nonrepresentational Muslim sacred art.

25. One of the most comprehensive overviews of religious reforming/ Reformation is a collection of essays, *The Reformation in National Context*, by a dozen prominent historians. Published by Cambridge University Press in late 1994 and edited by Bob Scribner, Roy Porter, and Mikulas Teich, the volume, because it is a collection of many voices, gives rich texture to the matter of reformation and certainly gives an

informing lens for viewing more acutely the shifts that are afoot now within our own time and place.

26. Among the first gestures of reformation always is, indeed, the "looking back" process to ascertain what *was* and how it differs from *what has evolved*. Much of Christianity's "re-Semitization," as I have argued earlier, seems to me to be just exactly that process in action. Perhaps even more fascinating is the whole renewal movement taking place in American Judaism where the pressure to counter assimilation has been equaled, if not exceeded, by the urgency of American Jews to rediscover and relearn what it *was* to be Jewish originally, since *what it has become* seems increasingly arid and unsatisfying. There could be no greater testament to the strength of this process than the sales, for example, of books like *Jewish Literacy* (New York: Wm. Morrow, 1992) and, more recently *Jewish Wisdom* (New York: Wm. Morrow, 1994), both by Rabbi Joseph Telushkin.

27. It would be a mistake to assume that this phenomenon is limited to Christianity. Being far and away the largest of America's faith systems, Christianity's wrestling with the issues has certainly been dozens of times more visible. But there is, for instance, a division presently over the Koran in American Islam. Islam has always treated its central text as a divinely inspired, divinely dictated body of words that cannot even be translated without violation. Yet Ahmadiyya Anjuman Ishaat Islam Lahore, USA, a fairly new publishing house in this country, exists primarily to publish a variant edition of the Koran that has now become the text preferred by the Nation of Islam, among others.

28. Once again it is possible to confirm the same patterns in magazine as well as book sales activity. For example, Barbara Goodwin, account executive at Eastern Periodicals, one of the country's larger magazine distributors, told me in October 1994 that *Biblical Archeology Review* had enjoyed a 500 percent increase in sales through Eastern from 1983 through 1993 because, she said, of "the public's interest in the category."

29. For a more detailed look at these titles and lists, see Bob Summer, "The Dead Sea Scrolls: A Publishing Gold Mine," *Publishers Weekly,* January 10, 1994, pp. 27–30.

30. *The Five Gospels* (New York: Macmillan, 1993) is part of the ongoing work of the Jesus Seminar and was written by the Jesus Fellows who constitute the scholarly working body of the seminar. Located in Sonoma, CA, the seminar includes such men as Marcus Borg and John

Dominic Crossan, is currently producing a new translation of Christian Scripture, and maintains its own publishing house, Polebridge Press, for the dissemination of its work. Another recent title coming out of the work of the same group of scholars and enjoying brisk sales is *The Complete Gospels* (San Francisco: HarperSanFrancisco, 1994).

31. These men are most currently represented by *Jesus: A Revolutionary Biography* (San Francisco: HarperSanFrancisco, 1994) [Crossan]; *Meeting Jesus Again for the First Time* (San Francisco: HarperSanFrancisco, 1994) [Borg]; and *The Death of the Messiah,* vols. 1 and 2 (New York: Doubleday, 1994) [Brown].

Chapter 9

1. This cataloguing is my own, though it does not differ substantially, I trust, from that of others.

2. The enormous popular appeal of these writings should not be underestimated. Hubbard's works, which continue to pour posthumously out from the publishing arm of the Church of Scientology, are perennial bestsellers constantly on one bestseller list or another.

There is also a push among others of the "Other" to reach out beyond their own constituencies with popularized presentations of their materials. The Church of Christ, Scientist, for example, decided in 1994 to release, through its publishing arm, the Christian Science Publishing Society, the major writing of Mary Baker Eddy, *Science and Health,* for the first time in popular or popularized form. The book was released on October 1, 1994, and had by October 10 already gone back for a second press run. An official for the Publishing Society attributed the public excitement and interest to changing times in the culture at large and to greater willingness on the part of the church to make itself accessible to "a shift toward availability that had previously been nonexistent in the Church and its members."

3. Woodward, "Dead End for the Mainline?" (see chap. 8, n. 15)is an excellent and succinct analysis of the present state of American Protestant Christianity in general.

4. Cox, *Fire from Heaven* (see chap. 2, n. 4), is cautionary in reminding us that "what we call 'pentecostalism' is not a church or even a single religion at all, but a *mood*" (p. 116 passim); and he speaks frequently of the need to see Charismatic Christianity as characterized by

a distinct but loosely similar set of proclivities frequently incorporated into a more mainline or traditional theology and/or praxis. He also is sensitive to the desire on the part of many adherents to each of those two modes of seeing to have those distinguishing differences recognized and honored.

On the other hand, however, we must not assume that such distancing is inherently part of either Pentecostalism or Charismatic Christianity nor that it informs all of their various constituencies. It is, for instance, interesting to note that when in October 1994 the old Pentecostal Fellowship of North America voted itself out of existence in order to make way for another, multiracial national organization, it chose to name that new group the Pentecostal/Charismatic Churches of North America.

5. On this I have only the proof of my own ears. I was listening with half my attention when suddenly I heard a male telecaster, name unknown, say these words.

6. For a particularly clear introduction to the possibilities of this new alliance, see Keith A. Fournier, with William D. Watkins, *A House United? Evangelicals and Catholics Together — A Winning Alliance for the 21st Century* (Colorado Springs: NAV Press, 1994). Fournier is also one of the endorsers of the paper *Evangelicals and Catholics Together.*

7. As a case in point, Janette Oke, the first lady of inspirational fiction, has over 12 million copies of her novels presently in print, a show-stopping record for any author; and there is no sign of any slowing in her market, much less of its saturation. To look more globally, one has only to check the data of Spring Arbor Distributors, the nation's largest distributor to the trade of religion products. Spring Arbor shows a growth of faith fiction as a genre over the past decade of over 100 percent; that is, 4.3 per cent of product moved in 1984, compared to almost 10 percent of product in 1994.

8. Of all of the new shapes and contours of contemporary American Christianity, this one is the most visible, of course. In particular, the movement by adherents toward "community" churches and small "cell" groups for worship and study has already become the subject of much study. Less well-observed but perhaps more prognostic of future developments is the shift by established congregations to a corporate existence independent of any superstructure, denominational heritage, or ecclesial authority — to exercise, in other words, what Woodward "Dead End for the Mainline?" (see chap. 9, n. 15) calls a "determindedly antidenominational" stance. Robert Schuller, for example,

was instrumental in 1993 in forming Churches United in Global Mission, a loose confederation of about two hundred of the country's most vigorous and vital community or nondenominational churches for the purposes of networking and outreach, *but not those of doctrinal unity or administrative economy.* Other present or emerging trends, including those toward relational theology, antiauthoritarianism, and a higher emphasis on ecumenism and the like, militate for the distancing of political activism from sacred space and sacred speech.

9. My opinion is based not only on my own observations as an active and denominationally affiliated Christian but also on the opinions of others even more intimately involved in the machinations of institutional church. On September 22–24, 1994, for instance, there was a gathering just outside Chicago of seventy-five leaders from eleven of the mainline churches to discuss this very issue of whether and what might be the future of denominational Christianity in America. The Rev. William McKinney, dean of Hartford Seminary, in many ways set the tone of that meeting when he observed, "We continue to undergo the disestablishment of Protestant denominations.... It is irreversible. Denominational structures lack a center of gravity."

10. It is, in my opinion, important here to mention one more time the possibility that American monotheism may be an emerging integer and to mention as well that the role of absolute, as opposed to trinitarian, monotheism in Christianity is currently a source of theological tension. Especially in Pentecostalism does the old argument between Arian and Athanasian views of the godhead seriously threaten the unity of the body politic.

11. Millennial books are already a strong genre in the market, but not just in religion per se and not just as apocalypse, end-time, or prophecy literature. The more significant prognosticator of the present and increasing strength of this genre is probably its presence in parareligion and basic spirituality lists. For example, a major title for HarperSanFrancisco on its winter 1994 list was *The Millennium Whole Earth Catalog,* which as one might suspect is the newest presentation of an old and very successful friend, the original *Whole Earth,* which sold over 3 million copies and snagged a National Book Award in the process. The interesting thing is that the book's publishers saw the millennium as the best way to successfully exploit *Whole Earth*'s established reputation as an innovative book for innovative readers. The other interesting thing is that, based on sales to date, they appear to have been very, very right.

12. Thanksgiving — the humbling, curative, loving and love-generating act of being most completely thankful and of knowing oneself to be so and, most merciful of all, of having the means by which to say so — thanksgiving as an attitude of living and as a condition of the perceiving mind is perhaps the quintessential example of what I mean here.

Of all the necessary religious/spiritual/sacral graces, none had slipped, until very recently, so far away from us as had the art of constant thanksgiving. Even our most earnest (earnestness being, after all, a very American characteristic) spiritual seekers tended toward petition and toward search uninterrupted by the helplessness of gratitude. Yet that attitude which the Native American calls reverence and which many from other traditions recognize by the name of thankfulness has been, since the late eighties, a big part of the generalized appeal of Native American spirituality and a big factor in the remarkable sales that have accrued to books about its practices and attitudes.

The persistent presence of reverence/thanksgiving in such solidly positioned books would alone be enough to confirm my sense that thanksgiving as a religious and spiritual grace was on its way back to its rightful place in the new, post-Christian faith practices of America. Now, however, there is an even stronger indication not only that the need of the spirit to live thankfully will be met, but also that thankfulness is probably going to be the first of the lost graces to return more or less universally across the *whole* spectrum of our possibilities. Morgan, *Mutant Message Down Under* (chap. 3, n. 25) is my proof text.

Like Redfield, *The Celestine Prophecy* (see chap. 3, n. 25), *Mutant Message* was originally self-published by its author in a very modest fashion; but its "message" would not be contained. Essentially without backing or major advertising support, and certainly without sales and marketing support, *Mutant Message* spread across the American sensibility by word of mouth and, to quote reader after bookseller after librarian to whom I have spoken," because of its message." Having arrived on the bestseller lists all over the country and apparently across the entire panoply of America's various mind-sets, *Mutant Message* was bought in 1994 by HarperCollins, a move that seems only to have expanded even farther the audience buying and lauding its "message."

And what is the message that even the book's title so insists on? Certainly there are several parts to the complete message that the author/

protagonist is destined to bring back to us from her time in the Australian Outback with the aboriginal tribe called the Real People, but the pervading one is thankfulness. *Among the Real People, the reverence of our Native American becomes an expressed affection that is pure, unadulterated, and constant thankfulness.*